D0568296

New York's MASTER CHEFS

As selected by
Bon Appétit magazine

Written by Richard Sax

Photographs by
Nancy McFarland

The Knapp Press   Publishers   Los Angeles

Bon Appétit® is a registered trademark of Bon Appétit Publishing Corp. Used with permission.

Copyright © 1985 KQED/Golden Gate Productions

This book was published by:
The Knapp Press
5900 Wilshire Boulevard
Los Angeles, California 90036

Bon Appétit® is the registered trademark of Bon Appétit Publishing Corp. and is used with permission.

All rights reserved. No parts of this book may be reproduced, stored in a retrieval system or transmitted, in any form or by any means, electronic, mechanical, photocopying, recording or otherwise, without permission in writing from the publisher.

Library of Congress Cataloging in Publication Data

Sax, Richard.
    New York's master chefs.

    1. Cookery, International.   2. Cooks—New York (N.Y.)
I. Title.
TX725.A1S387   1985   641.5′09747′1   84–26153
ISBN 0–89535–090–4

On the cover: *Cima alla Genovese*

Printed and bound in the United States of America

First Edition
10   9   8   7

Book Design: Robin Murawski
Recipe Testing Associate: Sandra Gluck

Contents

Introduction

The thirteen master chefs presented here would be at home anywhere, yet each has chosen to work in New York, a city whose adventurous and demanding inhabitants seem to offer a special challenge to creativity. The chefs spoke to us at length about the importance of having a discriminating audience and, when offered this book as a forum for expanding that audience, each—with great enthusiasm—agreed to take part.

It was the responsibility of *Bon Appétit* magazine to nominate the chefs, and we compiled a list that would ensure the widest possible variety of cuisines, cooking techniques and methods. As a result, some of the chefs were selected because they are expert practitioners of the classics, others because they are innovators and trendsetters. You will find that their exclusive recipes for French, Italian, Chinese, Viennese, Middle Eastern and American specialties add up to an exploration of what is happening in New York's great restaurant kitchens today.

Each chef was asked to submit a current menu, and from this the editors selected four recipes. The result—a tasting menu of an appetizer or soup, main course and dessert—is a capsule course in a particular cuisine. But because what master chefs practice is as much an art as it is a science, adapting their recipes for the home kitchen is a particularly challenging task. The author, Richard Sax, a New York-based food writer and cooking teacher who has the respect and trust of these master chefs, has captured the philosophy and personality of each in introductory interviews. Sax and his assistant, chef Sandra Gluck, were the conduit from chef to printed page, and the thoroughly tested and clearly written recipes that follow are the result of their gifted participation in this project.

In the course of preparing this book we realized not how different these thirteen men and women are but how much they share: talent tempered by patience, stamina and generosity.

The Editors
Bon Appétit magazine

Andrée Abramoff
Andrée's Mediterranean

Unlike many chefs, who by the age of fifteen are already spending long hours in professional kitchens, Andrée Abramoff did not begin to cook until she was in her mid-twenties. "I grew up in Egypt. My grandmother was a marvelous cook, and from her I learned to love food—but she wouldn't tell me exactly what she was doing, and besides, as a teenager I was interested in boys, not cooking.

"I started cooking for my family. At that time, I was working in New York as an editor of scientific journals, and my husband, Charlie, loves good food. So I wrote to my mother, who was then living in England, and from her I learned all the wonderful things that my grandmother used to cook." Abramoff's family offered her a rich, varied heritage: her father is French, her mother Egyptian and her paternal grandmother Greek.

Word of Abramoff's soul-satisfying food soon spread, and friends of friends were eager to taste her special brand of home cooking, with its deft but subtle use of herbs, garlic and spices. "I opened a tiny space here, to cater parties and teach cooking classes. People began to say, 'This is so lovely, I'd like to have a private party right here.' So I started to cook dinners by appointment.

"Many of the choices I offered are still my most popular menu items today: striped bass in phyllo, shrimp with tomatoes and feta cheese, rack of lamb, moussaka, Cornish game hen or squab stuffed with bulgur, pine nuts and raisins." Then Patricia Wells wrote about the classes and dinners in the *New York Times*, and we became busy overnight."

Today, having run her intimate restaurant at capacity for several years, Abramoff has become a seasoned professional. Her cooking, however, still retains the hearty warmth of the home cooking that inspired her.

This menu opens with two appetizers whose preparation, while a bit intricate, is not difficult: there are buttery, cheese-stuffed phyllo bird's nests (of Greek origin) and Syrian- and Lebanese-inspired kobeba, crisp-fried bulgur shells stuffed with fish. For our main course, Abramoff roasts garlic-studded lamb shanks with vegetables and orzo (small rice-shaped pasta), the separate components melding together in a delicious and hearty finished dish. "Be sure to salt before cooking," the chef advises, strewing the lamb shanks with sliced onions and olive oil. "If the salt doesn't cook with the food, it can never be added later." Putting the finishing touches on a dessert *bûche* of chestnuts and chocolate, Abramoff announces, "This is something I only do at holidays and special parties. And I serve it in very small portions— it's *rich*, I'm warning you!

"I think a lot of the flavor in my food comes from my Se-

Chef Andrée Abramoff

phardic Jewish background," she explains. "The lemon juice, the slow-simmered dishes, spices like cumin and coriander. Some of the best things I've ever tasted were Sephardic, and I've incorporated some of that food into my menu: calf's liver with rosemary, garlic and vinegar, the roast chicken my grandmother made on Friday night, the flourless chocolate walnut torte she'd make for the Passover seder. And she used to cook baby lamb ribs with spinach and peas; now, that's something!"

Abramoff's guests sense her commitment. The legend on an Egyptian tapestry in the dining room translates as, "Patience is the key to solace." "That," she says, "is for the people waiting for their food." Many of them, poking their heads into her kitchen to thank her after dinner, are surprised to find a work space that resembles a large home kitchen, rather than a stainless steel restaurant one. "We live upstairs," Abramoff laughs, delighted that food has become so central to her life. "I want to be able to have a home-cooked meal with my husband and family. Not enough people do that together these days. That's what food should be about: sitting down, having some wine; not gulping your food down, but taking time with it. It's a special feeling. After all, eating is fun!"

Menu

Bird's Nests with Cheese
Crisp flaky pastries filled with Parmesan, ricotta and Kasseri cheese

Kobeba Samakeyah
Deep-fried shells of bulgur stuffed with fish, served with Tahini sauce

Jarrets d'Agneau à la Greque
Lamb shanks roasted with onion, tomatoes and orzo

Bûche de Marrons au Chocolat
Chocolate chestnut log with whipped cream

Bird's Nests with Cheese

4 servings

Filling

2 eggs, lightly beaten
½ cup freshly grated Parmesan
  cheese
2 tablespoons ricotta cheese
2 teaspoons chopped fresh
  mint or ½ teaspoon dried
Pinch of freshly ground
  pepper

8 phyllo pastry sheets (about
  6 ounces)
½ cup Clarified Butter (see
  recipe, page 120)
¾ cup grated Kasseri cheese or
  crumbled feta cheese
8 Calamata olives (garnish)

1 *For filling:* In mixing bowl, combine eggs, Parmesan, ricotta, mint and pepper. Set aside.

2 Preheat oven to 375°F. Cut phyllo pastry sheets in half crosswise and cover with waxed paper and a lightly dampened kitchen towel. Place 2 half sheets of phyllo, one on top of the other, horizontally on work surface; trim off and discard a 1-inch strip from 1 short edge of sheets. Pull top sheet toward you so that it overlaps bottom sheet by about 1½ inches. Dot exposed surfaces with Clarified Butter.

3 Place a ½-inch-diameter dowel or no. 11 knitting needle about 1½ inches from long edge farthest from you. Fold edge over dowel. Spread about 1 teaspoon of filling along edge of folded flap. Fold dowel over filling; then carefully roll up phyllo toward you, leaving a 1½-inch strip at bottom edge.

4 Holding edges of the pastry at ends of dowel, gently press them toward center, forming pleats as you would on a curtain rod. (*Do not worry if some filling oozes out.*) Firmly holding ends of pastry to maintain pleats, carefully pull out dowel. Bring rolled edges of pastry around, forming a circle; the unrolled border will form bottom of each bird's nest.

5 Transfer bird's nest to ungreased baking sheet. Brush all exposed surfaces of pastry generously with Clarified Butter. Bake until golden, about 15 minutes. Remove baking sheet from oven and place about 1½ tablespoons of Kasseri in center of each nest. Return to oven until cheese is bubbly, 3 to 4 minutes. Place an olive in center of each nest. Serve hot.

Kobeba Samakeyah

4 to 6 servings

$^1/_2$ cup fine bulgur (cracked wheat)
$^1/_2$ small onion, cut in half
Salt and freshly ground pepper

Fish Filling
$^1/_2$ pound firm white fish fillets, such as flounder or cod
2 tablespoons ($^1/_4$ stick) unsalted butter
1 small or medium onion, chopped
2 scallions, trimmed and chopped
1 tablespoon chopped cilantro (coriander) (optional)

1 teaspoon ground cumin
Salt and freshly ground pepper

Tahini Sauce
$^1/_2$ cup tahini (sesame seed paste)
$^1/_2$ cup water (about)
2 tablespoons red wine vinegar
1 garlic clove, finely chopped
Salt and freshly ground pepper
2 tablespoons chopped parsley
Vegetable oil (for deep frying)

Jarrets d'Agneau à la Greque

Chopped onion and scallions are sautéed for the fish filling in Kobeba Samakeyah

1   Cover bulgur with water and soak 30 minutes. Drain and, a handful at a time, thoroughly squeeze out all liquid. Place bulgur, onion and salt and pepper in processor and process with on-and-off turns until nearly smooth, scraping down sides as necessary. Transfer to bowl and knead until smooth. Set aside.

2   *For fish filling*: Steam fish until just cooked. Flake into small pieces and set aside. Heat butter in a small skillet; add onion and scallions and sauté until onion wilts, 3 to 5 minutes. Stir in flaked fish, cilantro, cumin and salt and pepper, stirring gently over medium heat 2 minutes. Set aside and cool completely.

3   *For tahini sauce*: Place tahini and ¹/₂ cup water in processor or blender; blend until smooth. Add wine vinegar, garlic and salt and pepper; blend until smooth. Add enough water to bring sauce to pouring consistency. Transfer to small bowl; stir in parsley. Set aside, covered, at room temperature.

4   To assemble, place small bowl of ice water on work surface. Using palms, form golf ball–size balls of bulgur mixture. Dipping fingers in ice water as you work, shape each ball into a hollow tube around your index finger, gently pressing mixture into small cigar-shaped tubes about 3 inches long. Moisten fingers frequently and patch any cracks as you work. Slip each shell off your finger and fill with about 1 tablespoon of cooled fish filling, using a small spoon. Press ends of tubes over fish filling, forming a tight seal. Cover and freeze until firm, at least 2 hours.

5   Heat 2 inches of vegetable oil in large saucepan to 375°F. Fry kobebas until golden, 4 to 5 minutes, turning once. Serve immediately with tahini sauce.

Jarrets d'Agneau à la Grecque

4 servings

4 shanks (13 to 14 ounces each)
3 large garlic cloves, cut into slivers
Salt and freshly ground pepper
2 medium-large onions, sliced
³/₄ cup extra-virgin olive oil
¹/₄ teaspoon dried oregano
Pinch of cinnamon (optional)

1 pound fresh Italian plum tomatoes, peeled, seeded and coarsely chopped, or 2 cups canned Italian plum tomatoes with liquid, coarsely crushed
³/₄ cup dry white wine

2 cups Chicken Stock (see recipe, page 118)
1 cup orzo (rice-shaped pasta), preferably large

¹/₂ cup freshly grated kefalotiri or Parmesan cheese

1 Preheat oven to 400°F. Using sharp paring knife, remove as much of fat, sinew and translucent membrane as possible from lamb shanks. Insert garlic slivers into shanks, either by finding natural divisions in the meat or by cutting small incisions. Salt and pepper generously.

2 Arrange lamb shanks in roasting pan; strew onion slices over, then drizzle with olive oil. Roast 25 minutes. Sprinkle meat with oregano and cinnamon; spoon tomatoes on lamb, mounding on each shank. Pour white wine around meat. Return to oven and roast 45 minutes more.

3 Remove lamb shanks from pan and set aside. Add Chicken Stock to pan, stirring. Stir in orzo. Arrange shanks on top, baste them with some of stock, and return pan to oven. Cook until pasta is just tender and nearly all liquid has been absorbed, about 15 minutes. Remove from oven, cover pan tightly with aluminum foil, and let stand about 5 minutes. Serve hot with grated cheese.

Bûche de Marrons au Chocolat

12 to 16 servings

Andrée Abramoff spreads whipped cream over Bûche de Marrons au Chocolat

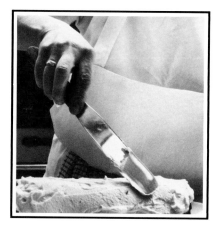

4 pounds fresh chestnuts or 2 pounds (about) whole unsweetened canned chestnuts, drained, or 4 cups canned unsweetened chestnut puree
³/₄ cup superfine sugar
¹/₂ cup (1 stick) unsalted butter, melted
2 to 3 tablespoons Calvados, applejack or Cognac
¹/₂ teaspoon vanilla

8 ounces semisweet chocolate (preferably Maillard), melted and cooled

Garnishes
1 cup whipping cream
1 teaspoon sugar
¹/₂ teaspoon vanilla
1 ounce semisweet chocolate, melted and cooled
1 tablespoon unsweetened cocoa
Candied violets

1 If you are using fresh chestnuts, cut an X on the flat side of each chestnut. Place in saucepan, cover with cold water and bring to boil. Cover and boil gently until tender, about 15 minutes. Remove pan from heat and let stand 15 minutes. Shell chestnuts, removing both hard outer shell and inner brown skin. If using canned chestnuts, simply drain. Reserve 3 whole chestnuts for garnish.

2 Puree chestnuts in a processor until very smooth. Add ³/₄ cup superfine sugar, butter, Calvados and ¹/₂ teaspoon vanilla; puree again

Bûche de Marrons au Chocolat

until smooth and fluffy. Add 8 ounces melted chocolate; puree until very smooth.

3 Line 4-cup round log-shaped mold or loaf pan with plastic wrap, pressing it until smooth. Pour in chestnut-chocolate mixture, tamping mold down to eliminate air bubbles. Smooth surface, cover with plastic wrap and refrigerate overnight.

4 *To garnish*: Unmold log on serving plate, carefully removing plastic wrap. Whip cream with 1 teaspoon sugar and ½ teaspoon vanilla until stiff; spread cream evenly over all sides of log, forming barklike ridges with spatula or decorating comb. Drizzle thin lines of chocolate down length of log, using paper pastry cone or fork. Roll the 3 reserved chestnuts in cocoa and arrange on log lengthwise; garnish with candied violets and refrigerate until serving. *May be refrigerated for up to 1 week.*

Lidia Bastianich
Felidia

Lidia Bastianich and her husband, Felix (Felidia, both name and restaurant, combines the talents of both) are natives of Istria, the peninsula that juts into the Adriatic south of Trieste. Istria has belonged to the Romans, Venetians, the Austro-Hungarian Empire, Italy and, since World War II, Yugoslavia. All of these influences can be felt in the cuisine, and this variety—plus a respect for good basic ingredients—is what makes the food at Felidia so exciting.

The Austrian influence is seen in dishes that use sauerkraut, such as *jota*, a lusty soup of beans, sauerkraut, potatoes and pork stock. Hungarian-inspired items include *palacinke* and plum-filled potato gnocchi rolled in fried breadcrumbs and cinnamon sugar; other dishes reflect Slavic and Venetian heritages. And tomatoes are generally used in paste form in Istria, rather than whole.

Bastianich came to New York when she was twelve. "I learned to cook from my grandmother," she says. "My mother worked at that time, and she would leave all the ingredients for dinner. I had to cook every night so I got plenty of practice."

The couple ran a restaurant in Queens for fifteen years, then opened Felidia nearly four years ago. "The audience you have in Manhattan—they are so knowledgeable. I can cook whatever is in season, and people here just love it."

Apparently, everyone else does, too. In June 1984 a panel of food authorities voted Felidia one of America's twenty-five best restaurants. This is particularly impressive when you consider that not a single Italian restaurant was selected five years ago.

Many homespun traditions are still maintained here: Felix cures the sweetest, silkiest prosciutto imaginable, and he and Lidia also make sausages, put up grapes and cherries in grappa, and even bake their own *foccacia* (flatbread), which is brought to each table at the beginning of the meal. But chances are that the visitor to Felidia will first rave about the pasta. Nowhere else in this country will you find pasta so finely rolled, so sheer, so tender to the bite, yet with plenty of body and rich egg flavor. "This is a poor man's pasta," Bastianich explains. "Most recipes don't include water, but that is what makes it so light."

Many diners here look forward to a mixed plate of such pasta specialties as *fuzi*, small diamond shapes sauced with meat, game or fowl; *pasutice*, folded pockets served only with fish sauces; and *pappardelle*. Felidia employs two cooks (one of them a woman from Istria) who do nothing but make the pasta.

Italians have long known that in the kitchen, simple is best. "Now," Bastianich remarks, "a lot of professionals are getting back to this basic home cooking. Taste this cherry-flavored grappa—it hits the palate with a pure taste. Food should be headed that way. When you cook, it's basic. You're in touch with life itself."

Chef Lidia Bastianich

Menu

Cima alla Genovese
Cold veal breast with a stuffing of vegetables and eggs, served with salsa verde

Pappardelle with Boneless Duck in Sguazet
Wide homemade noodles with a sauce of nuggets of boneless duck, chicken livers and porcini mushrooms

Red Snapper in Brodetto with Polenta
Red snapper in a rich tomato-wine broth, served with polenta

Fresh Cherries or Grapes in Grappa
Fresh fruit preserved in brandy, served after dinner

Cima alla Genovese

10 to 12 servings

Stuffing
- $^1/_2$ cup olive oil
- 1 medium onion, halved and sliced vertically through the root end
- $1^1/_2$ medium carrots, peeled, and cut into 3 x $^1/_4$ x $^1/_4$-inch julienne
- $1^1/_2$ zucchini, cut into julienne to match carrots
- $1^1/_2$ medium red bell peppers, cut into julienne to match carrots
- 2 cups spinach leaves, stems removed, shredded into $^1/_2$-inch-wide ribbons
- 1 cup fresh or frozen peas, thawed
  Salt and freshly ground pepper
- 14 eggs
- 2 cups freshly grated Parmesan cheese
- 4 ounces prosciutto or cooked ham, cut into julienne to match carrots

1 6- to 6$^1/_2$-pound breast of
  veal, boned, trimmed and
  butterflied, about 4$^1/_2$
  pounds
5 hard-cooked eggs, peeled

Poaching Liquid

$^1/_4$ cup coarse salt (about)
1 onion, sliced
1 carrot, sliced
3 bay leaves

Salsa Verde

3 tablespoons plus 1 cup
  extra-virgin olive oil
$^1/_2$ cup finely chopped shallot
4 anchovy fillets, chopped

$^1/_2$ cup red wine vinegar
  Salt and freshly ground
  black pepper, to taste
2 red bell peppers, roasted or
  1 cup canned pimientos,
  finely chopped
1 medium-size red onion,
  finely chopped (about 1
  cup)
2 celery stalks, finely chopped
  (about 1 cup)
1 cup finely chopped Italian
  flat-leaf parsley (pack
  loosely to measure)
2 hard-cooked eggs, peeled
  and finely chopped

Cima alla Genovese

Vegetable-and-egg stuffing is spread on veal breast for Cima alla Genovese

1   *For stuffing*: Heat olive oil in a large skillet over high heat. Add vegetables and salt and pepper. Sauté, stirring occasionally, until just softened, about 5 minutes.

2   In mixing bowl, beat eggs with salt and pepper to taste until blended. Beat in Parmesan until smooth. Add eggs to skillet, stirring constantly. Lower heat and stir until scrambled and set. Transfer to bowl and cool to room temperature. Stir in prosciutto.

3   Cut piece of twine long enough to go around length of veal breast 5 times. Thread twine into butcher's needle, knotting far end. Open up breast of veal on work surface; it should measure 12 x 16 inches.

4   Spread half of cooled stuffing down length of veal breast, leaving a 2½-inch border on long sides. Press stuffing together compactly. Lay 5 hard-cooked eggs end to end down length of stuffing. Spoon remaining stuffing over eggs, pressing it compactly with your hands into high, narrow shape.

5   Pull needle with twine through a hole in center of one short end of veal. Gather together the 2 corners of this short end and sew end together, stitching from inside outward at 1-inch intervals. Now stitch together both long sides of veal breast, gathering them together and pushing the stuffing in as you stitch at 1-inch intervals. Sew together other short end, tying a knot as you sew it shut. Cut off string, leaving about 4 inches at end.

6   Lay large sheet of cheesecloth (about 2 x 3 feet) next to stuffed veal breast. Without picking up breast, flip it over carefully onto center of cheesecloth. Fold one long side of cheesecloth over length of breast, wrapping it firmly, but not tightly. Then fold short ends up, then second long side. Wrap twine around length of breast 3 or 4 times, then bring twine around breast crosswise in a spiral at 1½-inch intervals. Tie twine at one end of breast.

7   *To poach*: Choose a deep pot large enough to hold veal; fill halfway with cold water. Add about ¼ cup coarse salt, sliced onion, sliced carrot and bay leaves. Bring to boil, lower heat, and add veal. If necessary, add additional water to cover. Place a lid directly on veal breast to keep it submerged. Simmer 1 hour and 45 minutes.

8   *For salsa verde*: Heat 3 tablespoons olive oil in medium skillet. Sauté shallots and anchovies, stirring until shallots are softened, 2 to 3 minutes. Cool. In bowl, combine 1 cup olive oil, wine vinegar and salt and pepper to taste. Add shallot-anchovy mixture and remaining ingredients. Stir well, adjust seasoning and set aside.

9   When veal is cooked, transfer it to roasting pan. Cover with second pan and weight it to compact the roll. Cool to lukewarm or room temperature, 2 to 3 hours.

10 When veal is cool, remove outer twine and cheesecloth. Cut off the one knotted end of twine, and starting at other end, very carefully pull out stitching and discard. Trim off excess fat, without cutting into the filling. Cut into thick slices and serve with salsa verde. (Unused portion may be refrigerated and served cold.)

Pappardelle with Boneless Duck in Sguazet

6 servings

Pasta
3¹/₂ *cups all purpose flour*
 2 *eggs*
¹/₄ *teaspoon salt*
 1 *teaspoon olive oil*
³/₄ *cup warm water (about)*

Boneless Duck in Sguazet
 1 4¹/₂- *to 5-pound duck,*
    boned, excess fat removed,
    cut into 1-inch pieces
¹/₄ *cup olive oil*
    Salt and freshly ground
    pepper
 3 *medium onions, chopped*
    (about 2 cups)
¹/₃ *cup finely chopped pancetta*
    (Italian dry-cured unsmoked
    bacon) or bacon
    Salt and freshly ground
    pepper

¹/₂ *cup coarsely chopped*
    chicken livers
¹/₂ *cup dried porcini*
    mushrooms (about 1
    ounce), soaked in 2 cups hot
    water for 20 to 30 minutes
 2 *bay leaves*
 1 *small branch fresh rosemary*
    or 1 teaspoon chopped dried
 4 *whole cloves*
 1 *cup dry white wine*
 3 *tablespoons tomato paste*
 3 *cups Chicken Stock (see*
    recipe, page 118)

 1 *tablespoon salt*
¹/₄ *cup freshly grated Parmesan*
    cheese, plus additional

Lidia Bastianich cuts fresh pasta dough into pappardelle strips

1 *For pasta*: Place 3 cups flour on work surface. Make a well in center. Beat together eggs and salt and pour into well. Stirring eggs with your fingertips, gradually incorporate flour. When about half of flour has been incorporated, drizzle 1 teaspoon olive oil over egg-flour mixture and stir it in. Use a little of the remaining ¹/₂ cup flour to rub any sticky bits from your fingers. Continue to add unincorporated flour alternately with warm water, until you have worked in all the flour and just enough water to form a mass that is supple but not sticky.

2 Knead until very smooth and silky, about 10 minutes, adding flour if it becomes sticky, or a little warm water if too firm. Cover and let rest 30 minutes.

3 *For boneless duck in sguazet*: Pat duck dry. Heat ¼ cup olive oil in heavy large casserole over high heat. Add duck and sprinkle with salt and pepper. Cook over high heat, stirring often, until lightly golden, about 10 minutes. Strain off about ¾ of the fat (discard or reserve for another use).

4 Add onions and pancetta to casserole, sprinkle with salt and pepper, and sauté until golden, about 8 minutes. Add chicken livers and stir 2 minutes.

5 Meanwhile, strain soaked porcini mushrooms, reserving liquid. Rinse and chop coarsely; strain liquid through fine sieve or cheesecloth and set aside. To casserole, add porcini, bay leaves, rosemary and cloves; stir 5 minutes. Add wine and cook, stirring, until wine is nearly evaporated.

6 Add tomato paste and simmer 2 minutes, stirring to coat all ingredients. Add reserved mushroom soaking liquid and Chicken Stock; bring to boil. Lower heat, cover partially, and simmer 45 minutes. Remove bay leaves and any rosemary stems. Skim fat from surface and adjust seasonings.

7 Cut dough into 3 pieces. Roll out 1 piece on lightly floured board to thickness of ¹⁄₁₆ inch. Starting from end nearest you, roll dough around and around rolling pin until all rolled up. Cut dough down length of rolling pin, then cut into pappardelle strips about 1 x 5 inches. Repeat with remaining 2 pieces of dough. Place pappardelle on tray lined with floured cloth and let dry briefly, uncovered, in refrigerator.

8 Bring 5 quarts water to boil; add 1 tablespoon salt. Add pasta gradually, stirring with wooden spoon. Boil vigorously, uncovered, until just tender, 2 to 4 minutes. Drain well.

9 Immediately return pasta to empty pot with half of sauce and ¼ cup Parmesan, tossing gently over medium heat. Serve immediately on heated plates, topping with remaining sauce. Pass additional Parmesan; supply a pepper mill at table.

Red Snapper in Brodetto with Polenta

6 servings

Polenta
6 cups cold water
1 tablespoon unsalted butter
1 tablespoon salt
1 bay leaf
1½ cups cornmeal

Red Snapper in Brodetto
2 whole red snapper (2 pounds each) (striped bass, sea bass or monkfish may be substituted), cleaned
2 cups vegetable oil

1 cup all purpose flour
3/4 cup olive oil
1 cup finely chopped onion
1/2 cup finely chopped scallion
   (white part only)
   Salt

2 tablespoons tomato paste
1/4 cup red wine vinegar, plus
   more as needed
3 cups hot water
Freshly ground pepper

1   *For polenta:* In heavy saucepan, combine water, butter, salt and bay leaf. Pour in cornmeal in a thin stream, stirring constantly. Bring mixture to simmer, stirring constantly, over medium heat. Reduce heat to medium low. Continue to stir over heat until mixture is smooth, very thick, and pulls away from sides of pan, about 15 minutes. Cover and keep warm.

2   *For red snapper in brodetto:* With cleaver, cut each fish into 3 pieces, leaving head and tail on. Heat vegetable oil in skillet to about 350°F. Dredge pieces of fish in flour, shaking off excess. Cook, turning once, until lightly golden but not cooked through, about 5 minutes. Drain on paper towels; set aside.

3   In separate large skillet, heat olive oil over medium-high heat; add onion and scallion and sauté, tossing until lightly golden, about 5 minutes. Add fish in single layer; sprinkle with salt. Spoon tomato paste between pieces of fish and cook about 3 minutes, shaking pan occasionally.

4   Stir together vinegar and hot water; add to fish. Bring to boil; lower heat and simmer, uncovered, 2 to 3 minutes. Carefully turn pieces of fish. Increase heat to medium high and continue to cook just until fish is cooked through, about 10 minutes. Transfer fish and a mounded spoonful of polenta to warm serving plates. Boil sauce vigorously until slightly thickened; correct seasoning with salt, pepper and a few drops of wine vinegar, if needed. Pour over fish and serve immediately.

Fresh Cherries or Grapes in Grappa

Makes 1 Quart

1 1/2 pounds ripe cherries or 2
   large bunches unblemished
   Muscat or other grapes

1/3 cup sugar
2 1/2 cups grappa or brandy
   (about)

1   Choose largest and firmest cherries or grapes; clip off stems, leaving 1/8 inch on fruit. Fill a 1-quart glass jar with fruit; add sugar and enough grappa to cover. Cover and shake to dissolve sugar.

2   Place jar in sun with cover ajar; let stand 1 week.

3   Cover tightly and store in cool dark place at least 3 months.

Michel Fitoussi
24 Fifth Avenue

It's not easy starting out as a boy wonder. At twenty-three, Michel Fitoussi, a native of Annecy, France, became chef of The Palace, a much-talked-about Manhattan restaurant. It was billed as the most expensive restaurant in the world, where diners paid as much as $150 per person for a twelve to fourteen-course feast. Fitoussi quickly garnered a reputation as a wildly extravagant showman in the kitchen, one capable of dazzling technical feats. "I felt I had to justify the prices," Fitoussi explains, "so I made pulled sugar baskets, clipper ships from bread dough and a six-tiered bird cage woven from pasta dough.

"And the ingredients! White truffles, black truffles, three two-kilogram cans of Beluga caviar every couple of weeks. When the *New York Times* wrote an article on foie gras, they included me as one of the experts. Can you imagine? I was only twenty-five years old. I was considered an 'expert' because I was using it like it was butter!"

But Fitoussi did much more than just make food look good. His nouvelle cuisine–inspired sauces were silky and delicate; he invented the white chocolate mousse, a difficult-to-perfect specialty that has since appeared on menus throughout the world.

After spending seven years at The Palace, Fitoussi moved to 24 Fifth Avenue, a Greenwich Village restaurant whose glassed-in sidewalk terrace affords a spectacular view of the Washington Square Arch at night. "Now I am more relaxed, more mellow, and my cooking is, too. Here, there is a different psychology of food. What is in the market determines the menu. I have something for everyone. I do 'gastronome food,' like baby pheasant with pesto stuffed under the skin, mallard duck with ginger sauce, and goose liver just sliced and seared in a hot, dry pan—it comes out crusty on top, rare in the middle.

"But I also do recipes for people who want something light. There is shrimp with caramelized pecans, and a coho salmon with cucumber sauce, made without butter."

Fitoussi opens and concludes his menu with two dishes that show his knack for beautiful constructions: a puff pastry cornucopia overflowing with bright jade asparagus and a chocolate mousse "flowerpot" guaranteed to delight and amuse even the most confirmed chocolate addict.

In a bravura performance, he demonstrated one of his most breathtaking creations: an apple spun of pure sugar syrup. He blew the crystal-sheer hollow form, then quickly pierced two holes in the shell, one to let air out, one through which to pipe in a tart lime mousse. "There," Fitoussi said. "That's in honor of the Big Apple."

Chef Michel Fitoussi

Menu

Asparagus Cornet with Lemon Dressing

Puff pastry cornucopia filled with fresh asparagus, served with lemon dressing

Ravioli with Sweetbreads

Sweetbread-stuffed ravioli in cream, garnished with sweetbreads in bordelaise sauce

Long Island Duck with Grapefruit

Crisp roast duck with grapefruit sections and a grapefruit-flavored brown sauce

Chocolate Mousse Flowerpot

Chocolate mousse and a light custard in a flowerpot, topped with a chocolate flower

Asparagus Cornet with Lemon Dressing

4 servings

½ pound Puff Pastry (see recipe, page 119)

Lemon Dressing
2 egg yolks
2 teaspoons Dijon mustard
Juice of 1 lemon

Salt and freshly ground white pepper
1 cup extra-virgin olive oil

1 pound fresh asparagus, preferably thin, stalks, bottoms trimmed

1 Roll pastry on lightly floured work surface to 3 x 20-inch rectangle, ¼ inch thick. Cut rectangle into 4 long strips, each ¾ inch wide. Wrap each strip around long metal cone (can be made from heavy-duty aluminum foil), beginning at tip and rolling strip around and around, overlapping slightly. Place on ungreased baking sheet and refrigerate 1 hour or more.

2   Preheat oven to 375°F. Bake pastry cornets until golden, about 15 minutes. Cool briefly, then very carefully remove metal or foil cone.

3   *For lemon dressing*: Combine egg yolks, mustard, lemon juice and salt and pepper. Whisk in oil a drop at a time. When dressing begins to thicken, add oil 1 teaspoon at a time, then continue adding oil in a thin stream. Adjust seasonings to taste.

4   Cook asparagus, tied in bundles, in boiling salted water until just crisp-tender; drain. Pour a small amount of dressing on each serving plate. Place a cornet on top of dressing and tuck asparagus into cornets, fanning tips out.

Asparagus Cornet with Lemon Dressing

Ravioli with Sweetbreads

4 to 6 servings (3 dozen ravioli)

Filling
1 pair veal sweetbreads, about 12 ounces, membrane and connective tissue removed
4 ounces veal shoulder
1/2 small onion, halved
2 shallots, coarsely chopped
2 garlic cloves
1/2 teaspoon fresh thyme or 1/4 teaspoon dried
1 small bay leaf
2 tablespoons Cognac
Salt and freshly ground pepper

Pasta
1 1/2 cups durum or all purpose flour
1 teaspoon salt

2 eggs
2 egg yolks

Sauce
1 small onion, quartered
1/2 cup plus 2 tablespoons chopped shallot
1/4 teaspoon fresh thyme or pinch dried
2 bay leaves
Salt and freshly ground pepper
2 cups whipping cream or crème fraîche
1/2 cup Bordelaise Sauce (see recipe, page 60) or Veal Stock (see recipe, page 118)
Chopped parsley (garnish)

1 *For filling:* Preheat oven to 400°F. In meat grinder or processor, coarsely grind 4 ounces of sweetbreads, the veal shoulder, onion, shallots, garlic, 1/2 teaspoon thyme, small bay leaf, Cognac and salt and pepper. Transfer mixture to shallow baking dish and bake until firm, about 20 minutes. Cool.

2 *For pasta:* In processor, combine flour, salt, eggs and egg yolks until dough comes together in ball. Transfer to lightly floured work surface and flatten slightly with rolling pin. Divide into 4 pieces. Use pasta machine or rolling pin to roll each piece 1/8 inch thick.

3 *For sauce:* Place reserved sweetbreads in small saucepan; add cold water to cover. Add onion, 2 tablespoons shallot, 1/4 teaspoon thyme, 2 bay leaves and salt and pepper. Bring to boil; reduce heat and simmer 8 minutes. Remove pan from heat and let cool. Drain sweetbreads and remove all connective tissue; separate into bite-size pieces.

4 Place 1 sheet of dough on ravioli form or work surface. Dot with 18 teaspoonfuls of filling placed 1 inch apart. Using a pastry brush dipped in cold water, moisten dough between mounds of filling. Gently lay a second sheet of pasta on top, pressing between mounds of filling to seal. Cut into neat squares. Repeat, using remaining 2 sheets of pasta and remaining filling. Set aside on lightly floured baking sheet.

5   Preheat oven to 450°F. Bring cream and remaining ½ cup chopped shallot to simmer; set aside. Cook ravioli in large pot of boiling salted water for 2 minutes. Drain and immediately transfer to wide, shallow baking dish. Pour cream and shallot over and bake until cream is bubbly and has thickened slightly, 5 to 8 minutes.

6   Meanwhile, place trimmed sweetbreads and Bordelaise Sauce or Veal Stock in small saucepan. Simmer, uncovered, until reduced to syrupy consistency.

7   Transfer ravioli and cream to warm serving plates. Spoon a few pieces of sweetbreads with their sauce into center of each portion. Sprinkle with chopped parsley and serve immediately.

Long Island Duck with Grapefruit

4 servings

2 Long Island ducklings
  (about 5 pounds each)
2 grapefruit
¼ cup sugar
⅓ cup red wine vinegar
3 cups duck stock* or Veal
  Stock (see recipe, page 118)

Blanched vegetables
(optional garnishes), such
as green beans, asparagus,
broccoli florets or julienne
of carrot, zucchini or turnip,
tied into bundles with strips
of blanched leek

Michel Fitoussi ties a bundle of blanched green beans with strips of blanched leek to garnish Long Island Duck with Grapefruit

1   Place duck, uncovered, in refrigerator for 4 days to dry out skin.

2   Preheat oven to 500°F. Cut off tail and excess neck skin from ducks and remove all excess fat. Place breast up on a rack in roasting pan. Tuck wing tips under. Roast until crisp and well browned, about 1 hour.

3   With sharp paring knife, remove thin slice from top and bottom of each grapefruit, then remove grapefruit skin in long strips. Set aside. Cutting between membrane, cut grapefruit into sections and set aside.

4   Place sugar and wine vinegar in heavy-bottomed saucepan. Cook over medium-high heat until vinegar has evaporated and sugar has caramelized lightly. Carefully add stock; bring to boil and simmer for 5 minutes. Add grapefruit skin and simmer 3 minutes longer. Strain into clean saucepan and simmer until reduced enough to coat a spoon lightly. Adjust seasoning with salt and pepper; keep warm.

*Prepare duck stock according to the procedure for Veal Stock, roasting bones and vegetables until well browned, then simmering about 3 hours. For an especially rich stock, roast duck bones and carcasses in a 450°F oven about 30 minutes, then transfer them, draining off all fat, to pan of simmering Veal Stock; simmer 15 minutes or longer.

5 Transfer duck to work surface. Run sharp knife under wishbone at front of breast, then carefully slip knife between each breast half and carcass. Cut boneless breast half together with the leg with thigh attached from duck in 1 piece. Repeat with remaining portions.

6 Lightly coat warm serving plates with sauce. Place duck over sauce; arrange grapefruit sections, overlapping, on top. Garnish with blanched vegetables as desired, and serve, passing remaining sauce separately.

Chocolate Mousse Flowerpot

10 servings

Crème Anglaise
- *3 cups milk*
- *1 cup whipping cream*
- *10 egg yolks, room temperature*
- *1 cup sugar*

Chocolate Mousse
- *¹/₂ cup sugar*
- *¹/₂ cup water*
- *4 egg whites, room temperature*
- *¹/₄ teaspoon cream of tartar*
- *2 cups whipping cream,*

whipped to soft peaks
- *1 cup unsweetened cocoa*
- *4 ounces semisweet chocolate, melted and cooled to room temperature*
- *3 tablespoons instant espresso powder*

Chocolate Flowers
- *10 ounces coating chocolate or milk chocolate, coarsely chopped*
- *¹/₄ cup light corn syrup*

1 *For crème anglaise*: Bring milk and cream to boil in heavy saucepan. Meanwhile, beat egg yolks and sugar in mixer until pale yellow and forms a ribbon when beaters are lifted, about 7 minutes. Slowly pour 1 cup of hot liquid into yolks, beating constantly. Transfer yolk mixture to milk and cream in saucepan and stir constantly over medium-low heat until it thickens enough to coat the back of a spoon; *do not boil.*

2 Strain into a large bowl set into a larger bowl of ice water and cool to room temperature, stirring occasionally. Cover and refrigerate at least 2 hours.

3 *For mousse*: Heat sugar and water in heavy saucepan over medium-low heat until sugar dissolves, stirring occasionally and brushing down any crystals from sides of pan with brush dipped in cold water. Increase heat and boil until mixture registers 240°F (soft ball stage) on a candy thermometer.

4 Meanwhile, beat egg whites and cream of tartar until soft peaks form. Slowly pour in hot syrup, beating until mixture is cool, about 5 minutes. Gently fold in whipped cream, cocoa, melted chocolate and espresso. Cover and refrigerate 1 hour.

Chocolate Mousse Flowerpot

5   *For chocolate flowers*: Line a jelly roll pan with waxed paper. Melt chocolate with corn syrup, stirring until smooth. Pour into prepared pan and spread with metal spatula to thickness of ¼ inch. Cool to room temperature.

6   Transfer paper with chocolate to work surface. Place second sheet of waxed paper over chocolate. Roll chocolate to ⅛-inch thickness. Cut into twenty 1-inch rounds with a cookie cutter. Roll 1 chocolate round into tight funnel shape for center of flower. Gather 3 more rounds around center, forming petals. Squeeze together at base. Place on waxed paper–lined plate. Repeat with remaining chocolate, forming 5 flowers. Refrigerate until flowers are firm.

7   To assemble, divide crème anglaise among five 2-cup cachepots or other porcelain dishes shaped like flowerpots. Top with chocolate mousse, mounding slightly in center. Set chocolate flower atop each (to anchor flowers more securely, place on lollipop sticks, then insert in mousse). Refrigerate until 20 minutes before serving. Each flowerpot makes 2 servings.

Larry Forgione
An American Place

While there has been much talk about the new American cuisine, what has been happening in American cooking is actually more an evolution than a revolution. No chef has been more closely identified with the rediscovery of our American roots than Larry Forgione, first at New York's River Café and now at his own restaurant, An American Place (named for Alfred Stieglitz's gallery of the 1930s).

While Forgione has always displayed solid technique, making imaginative recombinations of traditional themes, what is most striking about his cooking is his commitment to finding and using top-quality American ingredients from all parts of the country: Willapa Bay oysters, blue cornmeal, Michigan buffalo. It didn't all happen at once, though. When he graduated from the Culinary Institute of America in 1974, he recalls, "there was no real future for an American; all the kitchens, even here, were European controlled. The Europeans thought Americans didn't know anything about food. So I went to work at The Connaught in London to get enough training to get my foot in the door.

"I was struck by all the great ingredients that were brought in: the chanterelle mushrooms, the game birds. Well, we've got every possible climate in America, and I realized that these wonderful ingredients *must* exist here—it's just a question of finding them.

"I made a connection with someone with a shooting preserve who provided ducks fed on wild grasses. And I found a farm that raised chickens the way chickens are supposed to be raised, ranging free. Now they supply every top restaurant in the city—French restaurants, too. I think the first place they supplied, other than mine, was Lutèce."

Forgione's real breakthrough in ingredients came when he met a former Broadway actor, Justin Rashid, who had moved to Michigan. "Anything I wanted he would get: wild watercress, wild blackberries, wild huckleberries. It was the perfect solution: He was in a depressed area, and here I was asking the farmers there to convert acres to growing miniature vegetables and everything else—guaranteeing that I'd buy it all."

Working with such native-grown ingredients, Forgione has developed a highly distinctive style. His terrine of three smoked fish, garnished with their respective caviars, is a tour de force. And the chili-corn sauce served with steaks of beef or buffalo uses flavor combinations found in traditional recipes for chili.

Asked about the discrepancies between his cooking, with its refined overlay of professional technique, and traditional American home cooking, the chef remarks: "What I try to do is to highlight American ingredients, not my style of cooking. Of course, like all movements, it goes through a period when, if

Chef Larry Forgione

anything, it's *too* creative. But since opening An American Place, I feel much calmer with myself.

"Now maybe I'm becoming a little more rustic. When you first sit down, there's raised cornmeal bread, spicy pepper bread, and butter from a small family dairy farm in Michigan. And for dessert I make chocolate pudding or my Apple Pan Dowdy.

"Until recently," he continued, "we denied our past. It almost seemed that we were ashamed of American cooking. It's not easy to find our regional cuisines, but it's important that we do. Until now, no one was proud enough to do it."

Menu

Terrine of America's Three Smoked Fish with Their Respective Caviars

Fish terrine with a mousse of fresh fish and smoked white fish, smoked sturgeon and smoked salmon, served with a sour cream sauce and garnished with whitefish, sturgeon and salmon caviars

California Goat Cheese Crepes with Sweet Onion Sauce

Herbed crepes stuffed with goat cheese, olives and fresh basil, served with a sweet onion sauce

Michigan Beefsteak with Chili-Corn Sauce

Sautéed steak with a chili-flavored sauce flecked with bell peppers and corn kernels

Apple Pan Dowdy

Rum-laced apples topped with crisp bread rounds, baked in individual serving dishes

Terrine of America's Three Smoked Fish with Their Respective Caviars

Prepare this terrine one day before you plan to serve it.

12 to 16 servings

Mousse

1 1/2 pounds firm fresh white fish fillets (such as monkfish or halibut), trimmed and cut into chunks

1/2 pound smoked whitefish, cut into chunks

2 egg yolks

3 egg whites

2 cups whipping cream

1/2 cup chopped parsley

6 drops hot pepper sauce

2 teaspoons salt
Pinch of freshly ground white pepper

1 1/4 pounds smoked salmon, chilled and cut into 1/2-inch-thick slices

1 1/4 pounds smoked sturgeon, chilled and sliced into 1/2-inch-thick slices

Dressing

2 egg yolks

1 tablespoon cold water

1 cup plus 2 tablespoons vegetable oil

6 tablespoons white wine vinegar

2 cups sour cream

1/4 cup Champagne or dry white wine (optional)

2 teaspoons salt, or to taste

1/2 teaspoon freshly ground white pepper

Garnishes

2 hard-cooked eggs, shelled and cooled

1 small onion, finely chopped

1/4 cup chopped parsley

4 ounces golden caviar (fresh whitefish roe)

4 ounces fresh sturgeon caviar

4 ounces fresh salmon caviar

Smoked salmon and sturgeon are layered with a mousse of fresh fish and smoked whitefish for Terrine of America's Three Smoked Fish

1   *For mousse:* Process fish fillets, smoked white fish and egg yolks to smooth puree in processor, working in batches as necessary and scraping down sides occasionally. Add egg whites one by one, blending well. Gradually add cream, scraping sides of bowl as needed. Transfer mousse to bowl and place bowl in a larger bowl of ice. Stir in 1/2 cup parsley, hot pepper sauce, salt and pinch of pepper. Adjust seasonings to taste and chill well.

2   Lightly butter a 12 x 3 x 4-inch (preferably ceramic) terrine (a standard 9 x 3-inch loaf pan can also be used). Preheat oven to 350°F. Place well-chilled smoked salmon on work suface and split it down center, removing any small bones. Cut each half into rectangle about 2 inches wide and the length of mold, squaring off edges neatly. Cut two rectangles of smoked sturgeon to same size.

3   Use rubber spatula to spread 1/4-inch layer of mousse evenly over bottom and sides of mold. Lay one rectangle of smoked salmon down center. Spread a 1/2-inch layer of mousse over salmon, smoothing neatly.

Terrine of America's Three Smoked Fish with Their Respective Caviars

Top with layer of smoked sturgeon, then ¹/₂-inch layer of mousse; repeat until mold is filled, ending with smooth layer of mousse. Tap filled pan gently on work surface to eliminate air bubbles. Top with buttered aluminum foil, buttered side down. Wrap second layer of foil over top and place mold in a roasting pan.

4 Place pan on center rack of oven and pour hot water into roasting pan to come about halfway up outside of terrine. Bake 45 to 60 minutes, or until skewer inserted in center comes out clean (a 9 x 3-inch mold may take as long as 1 hour and 10 minutes). Remove mold from water bath and cool on rack.

5 *For dressing*: Place yolks and water in bowl of mixer and beat until creamy. Add oil very slowly. When about half of oil has been incorporated, begin alternating oil and vinegar, adding them in a thin stream. Whisk in sour cream briefly, then Champagne. Add salt and pepper and chill dressing, thinning, if necessary, with a little milk.

6 *To garnish:* Separate hard-cooked egg yolks from egg whites and chop each coarsely. Use a napkin to press whites and yolks separately through a sieve.

7 To serve, run a knife around edges of terrine, then unmold by inverting onto serving platter. Holding kitchen towel dipped in hot water over mold for a few seconds, lift off mold. Slice terrine with a knife dipped in cold water. Cover bottom of each chilled serving plate with dressing. Center a slice of terrine on each plate. Surround with ring of chopped egg yolk and egg white, onion and parsley. Place 6 small spoonfuls of caviar, 2 of each kind, over garnishes around plate. Serve immediately.

California Goat Cheese Crepes with Sweet Onion Sauce

4 servings

Crepes
1 cup all purpose flour
1 egg
1 egg yolk
1 cup milk, or more
  Pinch each of salt and
  freshly ground pepper
1 tablespoon chopped parsley
1 tablespoon chopped chives
2 tablespoons (¼ stick)
  lightly salted butter
  Olive oil

Filling
1 log California goat cheese (8
  to 10 ounces, about 1⅓
  cups), room temperature
2 tablespoons olive oil
3 tablespoons finely shredded
  fresh basil
2 tablespoons chopped parsley
2 tablespoons chopped black
  olives
  Freshly ground pepper

Sweet Onion Sauce
1½ tablespoons vegetable oil
1 medium onion, sliced
1 cup veal or beef trimmings,
  cut into ¾-inch dice
2 tablespoons dry vermouth
2 cups Veal Stock (see recipe,
  page 118)
2 tablespoons (¼ stick)
  unsalted butter, cut into
  small pieces
  Salt and freshly ground
  pepper

12 thin slices cucumber, skin
  scored along length of
  cucumber with a fork
  (garnish)
2 tablepoons plus 2 teaspoons
  finely slivered black olives
  (garnish)

1 *For crepes:* Sift flour into mixing bowl; add egg, egg yolk and a little of milk and stir to smooth paste. Gradually add remaining milk and mix until smooth. Add salt and pepper, 1 tablespoon parsley and

Larry Forgione spreads herbed crepes with goat cheese filling for California Goat Cheese Crepes with Sweet Onion Sauce

chives. Heat 2 tablespoons butter until it foams and turns very light brown; whisk into batter. Let stand at least 2 hours.

2   Thin batter with milk, if necessary, to consistency of whipping cream. Brush 7-inch skillet (preferably nonstick) with thin film of olive oil. Place over medium-high heat. When hot, add about 3 tablespoons batter and swirl to coat pan. Cook until lightly golden, about 1 minute; then flip and cook second side for 30 seconds. Continue with remaining batter, stacking crepes between sheets of waxed paper.

3   *For filling*: In mixing bowl, mash cheese with 2 tablespoons olive oil until soft and smooth. Stir in basil, 2 tablespoons parsley, olives and pepper.

4   *For sweet onion sauce*: In a heavy saucepan, heat vegetable oil over medium heat, then add onion and meat. Cook uncovered, shaking pan and stirring occasionally, until browned, about 20 minutes. Add vermouth, stirring; then add stock. Bring to boil and boil gently, skimming surface often until sauce has reduced to a light syrupy consistency, 30 minutes or longer. Remove from heat and swirl in 2 tablespoons butter bit by bit. Strain and season with salt and pepper.

5   To assemble, preheat oven to 375°F. Use a narrow spatula or butter knife to spread 1 side of each crepe evenly with about 2 tablespoons filling. Fold each crepe into quarters, pressing neatly. Blanch cucumber slices in boiling salted water 1 minute; drain well.

6 Arrange stuffed crepes in shallow baking pan, brush lightly with olive oil and place in oven until heated through, about 5 minutes. Warm sauce. Arrange 2 crepes, overlapping slightly, on each of 4 heated serving plates. Arrange 3 cucumber slices in a fan pattern next to crepes and garnish with finely slivered olives. Spoon sauce around crepes; serve immediately.

Michigan Beefsteak with Chili-Corn Sauce

4 servings

Chili-Corn Sauce
1 medium onion, top and bottom cut off and reserved
1 red bell pepper, top and bottom cut off and reserved
1 green bell pepper, top and bottom cut off and reserved
2 ears of corn, husked
4 tablespoons vegetable oil, or more
12 ounces beef stew meat (shin, chuck or round), cut into ³/₄- to 1-inch cubes
1 tablespoon finely chopped garlic
2¹/₂ tablespoons chili powder
Pinch of ground red pepper

Pinch of freshly ground black pepper
¹/₂ cup dry vermouth or dry white wine
4 cups Veal Stock (see recipe, page 118)
3 cups whipping cream
Salt
6 sirloin or rib eye steaks, boned and thoroughly trimmed (about ¹/₂ pound each after trimming)
5 tablespoons unsalted butter
2 tablespoons water
36 scallions (white part only), trimmed to 2¹/₂-inch lengths

1 *For chili-corn sauce:* Coarsely chop reserved trimmings from onion and from peppers; set aside. Cut whole onion and peppers into neat fine dice; set aside. With small paring knife, remove corn kernels, reserving cobs, and combine kernels with diced vegetable mixture.

2 In large heavy saucepan heat 2 tablespoons oil until very hot but not smoking. Add meat cubes and stir over high heat, shaking pan, until nicely browned, about 7 minutes. Add chopped vegetable trimmings and toss 4 to 5 minutes. Add garlic and toss 2 minutes. Add chili powder, ground red pepper and black pepper; stir 1 to 2 minutes. Add vermouth and reduce for 2 minutes. Add stock and reserved corncobs and bring mixture to boil, stirring.

3 Boil mixture gently, skimming fat from surface frequently, until stock has reduced to lightly syrupy consistency, 20 minutes or more. Add cream and continue to boil gently, skimming, until liquid is re-

Michigan Beefsteak with
Chili-Corn Sauce

duced to light sauce consistency (it will coat a spoon), 8 minutes or longer. Remove and discard corncobs. Strain half of mixture into clean saucepan, add corn-vegetable mixture to strained liquid, boil 2 minutes, and set aside. (Combine unstrained half and solids from strained half and reserve as a stew for another meal. Further cooking may be necessary.)

4   In large skillet, heat remaining 2 tablespoons oil until hot but not smoking. Working in batches if necessary, salt steaks lightly and sear them on both sides over high heat, about 1 minute per side. Using tongs to hold steaks, sear edges. Lower heat slightly and continue to cook steaks, turning them once, until rare, $4^1/2$ to 5 minutes total.

5   Meanwhile, in separate skillet, heat butter and water, shaking pan until they are blended. Add scallions and cook over high heat, shaking skillet constantly, until crisp-tender, about 2 minutes.

6   To serve, place a steak in center of each heated serving plate. Warm sauce and adjust seasonings to taste. Spoon some sauce around each steak. Place 3 scallions on each side of each steak. Serve immediately.

Apple Pan Dowdy

6 servings

Butter (for ramekins)
12 slices firm white bread
6 tablespoons (³/₄ stick) unsalted butter, or more Sugar
4 large baking apples (Rome or *other not-too-tart variety*), peeled, quartered, cored, quarters cut crosswise into ¹/₄-inch slices
3 tablespoons molasses
¹/₂ cup firmly packed light brown sugar

¹/₂ teaspoon cinnamon
¹/₄ teaspoon freshly grated nutmeg
2 tablespoons plus 2 teaspoons dark rum
2 tablespoons lemon juice
1 tablespoon vanilla
5 tablespoons unsalted butter, chilled and cut into small pieces
1 cup whipping cream, lightly whipped and sweetened with sugar

1 Preheat oven to 375°F. Butter six 8-ounce ramekins or soufflé dishes. Use a cutter to cut slices of bread into 12 rounds that fit into dishes. Spread rounds with softened butter on both sides; sprinkle 1 side with a little sugar. Place 1 bread round in each dish, sugared side down. Reserve 6 rounds.

2 Toss sliced apples with molasses, brown sugar, cinnamon, nutmeg, rum, lemon juice, vanilla and pieces of butter. Spoon mixture into dishes, filling them nearly full and spooning juices over. Top each dish with a reserved bread round, sugared side up.

3 Place ramekins in roasting pan, place pan on center rack of oven, and pour inch of hot water into roasting pan around ramekins. Bake until bread is golden brown, about 25 minutes. Serve warm in ramekins; serve whipped cream separately.

Andy Kisler
Vienna 79

In his mid-twenties, Andy Kisler is the youngest of the chefs in this book. A native of Vienna, he came to New York in 1982 to head the kitchen at Vienna 79. Breezing into the kitchen in a black leather jacket to begin the fifteen-hour day he puts in six times a week, Kisler sums up his new home: "New York? A crazy city—but good!"

Kisler arrived here well prepared. In the Old World tradition, he began his apprenticeship at fifteen. "You know," he comments, "if a chef says that he always knew he wanted to cook, I don't quite believe it. Who knows what he wants to do with his life at fifteen? At fifteen, you want to go to a disco." Kisler trained at Austria's Palais Schwarzenberg, cooked in Switzerland and at La Marée in Paris, and put in several years in the kitchen at Vienna's Hotel Sacher, home of one of the world's best-known desserts.

While Kisler enjoys cooking the traditional fare of his country, what excites him most is the lighter, streamlined fare that has all but taken over in the past few years, both at home and in the United States.

Working in a light vein, Kisler has devised a broad menu of seasonal specialties: medallions of lobster and langoustine in a Calvados cream sauce, a warm salad of marinated squab breast with grapes, crisp veal sweetbreads on a bed of greens. Even when preparing traditional dishes, he takes pride in the fact that "I never use any starch to bind sauces—no roux, no cornstarch."

In the menu that follows, Kisler offers a tasting sampler, working in several styles. The Wild Mushroom Soup, an earthy blend of dried cèpes and vegetables with a hint of Madeira, is closest to his mother's home cooking. For the fish course, Kisler suggested one of his lightest dishes, rapidly sautéed salmon fillets in a cream reduction flavored with anchovies and tomatoes.

Kisler pulls out all the stops for the main dish, Pheasant with Champagne Cabbage, which utilizes a variety of cooking techniques. He begins by removing the breast, leg and thigh portions from the pheasant; then he bones the legs, flattens them and stuffs them with a Port-flavored chicken mousse studded with a crunchy dice of root vegetables. When cooked to a golden brown, the pheasant is sliced and arranged on a bed of creamy caraway cabbage and napped with a light *jus* made from the reserved pheasant bones. The entire effect is warm and comforting, and not at all heavy—an elegant composition.

Dessert is one of Austria's favorites, *Salzburger Nockerl*. With these puffs of vanilla- and lemon-scented soufflé, Kisler brings the menu around full circle, back from a highly refined chef's creation to a traditional dish of his homeland.

Chef Andy Kisler

Menu

Wild Mushroom Soup
A hearty soup of wild mushrooms and vegetables, flavored with Madeira

Fillet of Salmon with Anchovies and Tomatoes
Sautéed salmon fillet with a light sauce of cream, anchovies and tomatoes

Pheasant with Champagne Cabbage
Boneless breast and leg of pheasant, stuffed with a vegetable-studded mousseline of chicken and served on a bed of Champagne cabbage

Salzburger Nockerl
Classic Austrian dessert soufflé flavored with vanilla and lemon

Wild Mushroom Soup

4 servings

4 ounces dried cèpes
2 tablespoons dry Madeira
Hot water, as needed
4 tablespoons butter ($^{1}/_{2}$ stick), preferably clarified (see recipe, page 120)
1 medium-large onion, chopped (about 1 cup)
1 tablespoon fresh marjoram or $^{3}/_{4}$ teaspoon dried
$1^{1}/_{2}$ teaspoons Sherry vinegar
$^{1}/_{2}$ teaspoon salt
2 tablespoons all purpose flour

4 cups beef stock (see recipe for Veal Stock, page 118)
1 cup whipping cream
$^{1}/_{2}$ carrot, cut into $^{1}/_{2}$-inch dice (about $^{1}/_{4}$ cup)
1 baking potato, peeled and cut into $^{1}/_{2}$-inch dice (about $1^{1}/_{3}$ cups)
Juice of $^{1}/_{2}$ lemon
Freshly ground white pepper
2 tablespoons chopped parsley

1 Soak cèpes in Madeira and hot water to cover for 20 to 30 minutes. Drain, reserving and straining soaking liquid. Rinse and drain cèpes; chop coarsely.

2 In saucepan, heat 2 tablespoons butter over medium-high heat, add cèpes, onion and marjoram and toss 2 minutes. Add vinegar, 1/2 teaspoon salt and 1/4 cup of reserved liquid. Simmer 5 minutes; set aside.

3 In separate saucepan, melt remaining butter; stir in flour and cook 3 minutes. Whisk in stock and bring to boil. Add cream and carrot and simmer, uncovered.

4 Meanwhile, blanch potato in boiling salted water 3 minutes; drain and rinse under cold water. When carrot is nearly tender, add potato and cook until all ingredients are tender, about 5 minutes. Add cèpe mixture and simmer 5 minutes. Add lemon juice and adjust seasonings to taste with salt and white pepper. Add parsley and serve.

Fillet of Salmon with Anchovies and Tomatoes

4 servings

1 pound salmon fillets, trimmed, skin removed, and cut on a slight diagonal into 2-ounce pieces
All purpose flour, preferably instant
1/4 cup (about) Clarified Butter (see recipe, page 120)
1/4 cup dry white wine
1/2 cup whipping cream
3 anchovy fillets, chopped

1/2 medium-size ripe tomato, cored, peeled, seeded and diced
3 tablespoons unsalted butter, chilled and cut into pieces
2 tablespoons chopped fresh chives
Salt and freshly ground pepper to taste
4 small cooked broccoli florets (garnish)

1 Pat salmon dry with paper towels. Dip 1 side of each piece in flour, shaking off excess. Heat Clarified Butter in large skillet over medium-high heat. Working in batches if necessary, sauté salmon floured side down, shaking skillet occasionally, until golden, 1 1/2 to 2 minutes. Carefully turn salmon and brown second side. Transfer to warm serving plates, blotting up any excess fat from fish. Keep warm.

2 Pour off butter from skillet. Add wine, scraping up any browned bits. Add cream, anchovies and tomato and boil until very lightly thickened, 2 to 3 minutes. Lower heat and swirl in butter, 1 or 2 pieces at a time. Add chives and adjust seasonings to taste. Pour sauce over fish; garnish with broccoli and serve.

Pheasant with Champagne Cabbage

Pheasant with Champagne Cabbage

If pheasant is not available, you can also prepare this with chicken.

4 servings

2 pheasants (about 2¹/₂ pounds each)

Pheasant Stock

3 tablespoons vegetable oil
1 onion, sliced
1 carrot, peeled, trimmed and sliced
1 celery stalk, trimmed and sliced
3 large shallots, sliced
2 ripe tomatoes, coarsely chopped
4 bay leaves
4 juniper berries, crushed

15 to 20 peppercorns
2¹/₂ cups dry red wine
1 cup water, plus more as needed

Mousseline Stuffing

¹/₂ chicken breast (about 5 ounces), boned, skinned and cut into 1-inch pieces
1 egg white
¹/₄ cup whipping cream
2 tablespoons Port
¹/₂ teaspoon salt
Freshly ground white pepper

2 tablespoons finely diced
carrot

2 tablespoons finely diced leek
(white part only)
2 tablespoons finely diced
turnips
1 1/2 tablespoons finely diced
celery root (celeriac)
2 medium mushrooms, diced
2 to 3 fresh sage leaves,
chopped, or pinch dried

Champagne Cabbage
3 tablespoons unsalted butter
1 medium onion, sliced
1 tablespoon sugar
1/2 head white cabbage, cored,
outer leaves removed,
shredded (about 4 cups)
1 apple, MacIntosh or Granny
Smith, peeled, cored and cut
into thin julienne

1 cup Champagne or dry
white wine
1 cup whipping cream
1 tablespoon white wine
vinegar
1 teaspoon caraway seed
1/2 teaspoon salt
Freshly ground black pepper

6 tablespoons Clarified Butter
(see recipe, page 120)

Sauce
1 tablespoon sugar
3 tablespoons gin
1 1/2 cups pheasant stock
3 tablespoons dry red wine
1/4 cup (1/2 stick) unsalted
butter, chilled and cut into
pieces
Salt and freshly ground
black pepper

1   With sharp boning knife, carefully remove each breast half from pheasants. Set breast halves aside. Remove legs with thighs attached. To bone each leg-thigh portion, use sharp boning or paring knife to slit leg and thigh meat, cutting parallel to bones. Carefully scrape thigh meat away from bone. Cut through joint between leg and thigh, keeping meat in 1 piece. Scrape away all remaining thigh meat and cut or pull out thighbone. Use cleaver to cut off knob end of leg. Scrape meat from bone and pull out bone. Refrigerate meat, covered. Reserve bones and carcasses.

2   *For pheasant stock*: Preheat oven to 450°F. Place vegetable oil in roasting pan with reserved bones and carcasses. Roast until well browned, stirring occasionally, about 30 minutes. Add remaining stock ingredients except wine; roast 10 minutes longer. Transfer solids to stockpot, discarding fat. Place roasting pan over high heat and add wine, scraping up all browned bits. Boil, stirring until wine is nearly evaporated; add 1 cup water; add liquid to stockpot. Add cold water to cover, bring slowly to boil, and skim well. Lower heat; simmer, uncovered, 3 to 4 hours. Strain, pressing down on solids to extract all liquid; discard solids. Cool to room temperature and refrigerate. When chilled, lift off solidified fat from surface and discard.

3   *For mousseline stuffing*: Puree chicken pieces in processor until smooth. Add egg white and process until smooth. With machine running, add cream in thin stream; then add Port, salt and pepper. Transfer to bowl; fold in remaining stuffing ingredients. Adjust seasonings to taste. Chill, covered.

4   To assemble, place leg-thigh portions, skin side down and short side toward you, between 2 sheets of plastic wrap; flatten gently with mallet or side of cleaver. Spread about ⅓ cup of stuffing on each portion and fold meat over to form a ½-inch border on each of 2 long sides. Starting with a short side, roll into a neat cylinder. Use kitchen twine to tie compactly, wrapping twine around once lengthwise and 3 times crosswise. Chill, covered, until firm, at least 30 minutes.

5   *For champagne cabbage*: Melt 3 tablespoons butter in large skillet over medium-high heat; add onion and sugar and cook, stirring constantly, until lightly golden, about 5 minutes. Add cabbage and toss for 3 minutes. Add remaining ingredients and lower heat to medium. Cook, uncovered, until cabbage is just tender and liquid is nearly absorbed, 20 to 25 minutes. Adjust seasonings to taste. Cover and set aside to keep warm.

Salzburger Nockerl

6 Preheat oven to 450°F. Heat 6 tablespoons Clarified Butter in large ovenproof skillet. Salt and pepper stuffed leg packages and sauté, shaking pan occasionally, until golden on all sides, about 4 minutes. Place skillet in oven and roast 4 minutes.

7 Return skillet to top of stove over medium-high heat. Add breast halves to pan, skin side up, and sprinkle with salt and pepper. Sauté 2 minutes, shaking pan occasionally. Turn breasts skin side down, sprinkle with salt and pepper and return to oven until everything is tender, about 7 minutes.

8 *For sauce*: Meanwhile, cook sugar, without stirring, in small heavy saucepan over medium heat until caramelized, about 4 minutes. Add gin and stock; boil until reduced by half. Add wine and return to boil. Lower heat and swirl in ¼ cup butter, 1 or 2 pieces at a time, until smooth. Adjust seasonings to taste with salt and pepper.

9 Transfer meat to work surface. Cut leg-thigh portions crosswise into ½-inch-thick slices. Thinly slice breasts lengthwise on a diagonal.

10 Mound about ½ cup of cabbage in center of each of 4 warmed serving plates. Place leg-thigh slices around bottom of each plate, overlapping slightly. Place breast slices in a fan pattern at top of each plate, overlapping slightly. Spoon some sauce around meat and cabbage; serve rest of sauce separately.

Salzburger Nockerl

4 servings

4 teaspoons currant or other
    jelly
4 tablespoons whipping cream
2 tablespoons (¼ stick)
    unsalted butter, cut into 4
    pieces
9 large egg whites

½ cup vanilla sugar (or ½ cup
    sugar plus ½ teaspoon
    vanilla)
Juice of ½ large lemon
4 egg yolks, lightly beaten
½ cup sifted all purpose flour

1 Preheat oven to 450°F. Place 4 shallow 9-inch oval gratin dishes on a baking sheet. In each, put 1 teaspoon jelly, 1 tablespoon cream and 1 piece butter.

2 In mixer, beat egg whites on medium-high speed until they form soft peaks. Gradually add vanilla sugar and lemon juice and continue to beat until stiff and shiny.

3 Use a large rubber spatula to gently fold egg yolks and flour into beaten whites. Use spatula to transfer 3 large mounds of mixture to each baking dish; shape and smooth them. Bake until puffed and golden, about 8 minutes. Serve immediately.

Stanley Kramer
Peter Roggensinger
George Morfogen
Oyster Bar and Restaurant, Grand Central Station

Chef Stanley Kramer (right) with seafood buyer George Morfogen and pastry chef Peter Roggensinger

Like the landmark Beaux Arts Grand Central Station in which it is housed, the Oyster Bar and Restaurant is an American institution. Ever since the restaurant opened its doors in 1913, commuters have packed the stand-up bar four deep to sample fresh-from-the-sea oysters and clams, either iced on the half shell or quickly simmered in a creamy pan roast. Patrons with a bit more time perch at counter stools, enjoying bowls of New England or Manhattan-style clam chowder, served with freshly made coleslaw and hot home-baked rolls. And in the enormous dining rooms, which are surprisingly cozy considering their proportions, guests have a hard time choosing from the long list of the day's catch on the lunch and dinner menus.

The Oyster Bar and Restaurant upholds the worthy tradition of the American seafood house: tables laid with red checkered cloths, sea salt, and addictive oyster crackers; hefty portions of simply grilled and fried fish and plenty of homemade desserts. But everything here is done a little bigger and a little better, and that makes all the difference.

Unlike many great restaurants, where the inspiration comes primarily from a single person in charge, the Oyster Bar and Restaurant is decidedly a team effort. At the helm are owner Jerry Brody and vice-president Mario Staub, with Chef Stanley Kramer in charge of the kitchen. Kramer is a good-natured veteran of some of New York's finest kitchens, his experience including five years cooking with the late Albert Stockli at The Four Seasons.

Kramer is a master at traditional fish cookery. But he has also devised heartier dishes in which firm-fleshed fish such as swordfish, lotte (monkfish) and mako shark are prepared in ways usually reserved for meat—sautéed, then sauced with quick pan reductions.

Peter Roggensinger, the Oyster Bar's Swiss pastry chef, spent three years working with Bruno Comin at The Four Seasons. He takes great pride in his picture-perfect dessert buffet, presenting some fifteen selections daily. While Roggensinger turns out excellent renditions of such down-home American treats as rice pudding, fruit pies and cheesecake, he is most eager for diners to try his half-dozen daily specials, which include a strawberry-almond galette, mousses and sorbets and the layered frozen parfait in this menu.

With simply cooked fish, freshness is everything, and the third major force in the Oyster Bar team is George Morfogen, the seafood buyer. Morfogen is at the wholesale seafood market by 3:45 each morning, selecting the three to four thousand pounds of fish served daily. "With fish, you've got to know what you're looking for," he explains. "First of all, fresh fish doesn't

smell 'fishy.' It should be firm to the touch, leaving no indentation when pressed. The eyes should be clean and shiny. And the fish should have a nice bright sheen, inside and out. No matter what kind of fish you buy, the best way to keep it fresh is to place it on a bed of ice in the refrigerator. Just refrigerating it can dry it out."

The freshest possible fish and shellfish, straightforward preparation, hearty portions, a one-of-a-kind atmosphere: the management at the Oyster Bar and Restaurant has had the good sense not to tamper with the basics. Under the careful guardianship of an expert team, these elements have kept diners satisfied for decades.

Menu

Oyster Pan Roast
Fresh oysters simmered in their own juices, with cream

Mako Shark Steak Au Poivre
Sliced mako shark coated with pepper, sautéed and sauced with a reduction of Cognac and cream

or

Tournedos of Lotte with Lobster and Lobster Butter
Sautéed slices of monkfish fillet, garnished with medallions of lobster, in a cream sauce enriched with lobster butter

Raspberry Honey-Almond Parfait
Frozen layered dessert of raspberry and honey-almond mousse

Oyster Pan Roast

Prepare each serving separately.

1 serving

2 tablespoons clam broth or juice
2 tablespoons (¹/₄ stick) butter
¹/₄ teaspoon paprika
Pinch of celery salt
1 tablespoon Worcestershire sauce

9 shucked oysters with their liquor
1 to 2 tablespoon chili sauce
¹/₂ cup half and half
1 slice toast
Pinch of paprika

1 In top of double boiler, place clam broth, 1 tablespoon of the butter, ¹/₄ teaspoon paprika, celery salt and Worcestershire sauce; stir gently. Add oysters and simmer just until their edges start to curl, about 1 minute. Stir in chili sauce and half and half and heat through.

2 Place slice of toast in warm bowl, pour oyster pan roast over toast, and float remaining tablespoon butter on top. Sprinkle with a pinch of paprika. Serve immediately.

Oyster Pan Roast

Mako Shark Steak Au Poivre

6 servings

12 thick slices mako shark (about 4 ounces each), skins removed
Salt and coarsely crushed pepper
½ cup Clarified Butter (see recipe, page 120)

2 to 3 tablespoons finely chopped shallot
⅓ cup Cognac, plus more as needed
2 cups whipping cream
2 tablespoons veal glaze* or ⅓ cup Veal Stock (see recipe, page 118)

1 Pat shark slices dry. Salt lightly. Arrange crushed pepper on plate or sheet of waxed paper; dredge each slice of fish in pepper, shaking off excess to leave light coating.

2 Heat Clarified Butter in heavy, large skillet until hot. Working in batches if necessary, sauté fish slices until crusty and lightly golden, 2 to 3 minutes per side. Transfer to warm serving plates, and keep warm.

3 Pour off all but about 1 tablespoon butter from skillet. Add shallot and toss briefly; carefully add ⅓ cup Cognac. Add cream, veal glaze and any juices from fish. Boil until reduced to consistency that will lightly coat the back of a spoon. Adjust seasoning with salt and pepper and a few drops of Cognac. Strain over fish and serve.

For veal glaze, boil ½ cup Veal Stock until very syrupy and reduced to about 2 tablespoons.

Tournedos of Lotte with Lobster and Lobster Butter

This recipe uses the lobster shells to make a large quantity of lobster butter. Store the extra butter in the freezer and use it in sauces, as in this recipe, or serve with broiled fish.

6 Servings

Lobster Butter
2 1- to 1¼-pound lobsters
2 tablespoons Clarified Butter (see recipe, page 120)
1 small onion, coarsely chopped
1 carrot, peeled and coarsely chopped
1 celery stalk, trimmed and coarsely chopped
1 garlic clove, peeled and crushed

1 sprig fresh thyme or ¼ teaspoon dried
1 sprig fresh tarragon or ¼ teaspoon dried
1 bay leaf
2 tablespoons Cognac
3 pounds (12 sticks) unsalted butter
⅓ cup tomato paste

Lotte and Sauce

18 pieces skinned lotte
   (monkfish) fillet (2 ounces
   each)
Salt and freshly ground
   white pepper

$^1/_2$ cup Clarified Butter
$^1/_4$ cup finely chopped shallot
$^1/_4$ cup Cognac
 2 cups whipping cream
   Parsley sprigs

1   *For lobster butter*: Steam or boil lobsters until just tender, 8 to 10 minutes. Cool, then remove all lobster meat from shells. Refrigerate meat, covered; set shells aside.

2   In large saucepan, heat 2 tablespoons Clarified Butter. Add onion, carrot, celery, garlic, thyme, tarragon and bay leaf; toss over high heat 3 minutes. Add lobster shells, stirring; then add 2 tablespoons Cognac and stir 3 minutes. Add butter and tomato paste and simmer gently, covered, 2 to 3 hours. Strain, pressing solids firmly. Set aside for 15 minutes. Skim any froth from surface and strain again through several layers of dampened cheesecloth, leaving behind any milky residue in

Tournedos of Lotte with Lobster and Lobster Butter

bottom of pan (discard residue). Cool, then chill or freeze in small containers.

3 *For lotte and sauce*: Pat lotte dry; sprinkle with salt and pepper. Heat ¹/₂ cup Clarified Butter in heavy large skillet over medium-high heat. Working in batches if necessary, sauté lotte until lightly golden, about 2 minutes per side. Scatter shallot around fish and cook 2 minutes longer. Pour in ¹/₂ cup Cognac and cook 1 minute longer. Transfer to warm serving plates and keep warm.

4 Add 1 cup cream to skillet and reduce by half. Add remaining cup and boil until thick enough to coat a spoon lightly. Lower heat and spoon in the ¹/₂ cup lobster butter a little at a time, whisking constantly.

5 Strain sauce into clean saucepan. Cut reserved lobster meat into thick slices and add. Simmer gently 2 minutes. Place lobster pieces between pieces of lotte. Nap with sauce; garnish with parsley and serve immediately.

Raspberry Honey-Almond Parfait

8 servings

Honey-Almond Parfait
¹/₂ cup whipping cream
1 egg
1 egg yolk
3 tablespoons honey
¹/₂ vanilla bean, split lengthwise, seeds removed and reserved, or ¹/₂ teaspoon pure vanilla extract
2 ounces sliced almonds (about ²/₃ cups), toasted (toast 10 minutes at 350°F) and cooled

Raspberry Parfait
14 ounces fresh raspberries (about 3¹/₂ cups), or 3 10-ounce packages frozen raspberries, thawed and drained
¹/₃ cup sugar
1 cup whipping cream

¹/₃ cup egg whites (slightly more than 2 large)
¹/₂ cup sugar
2 tablespoons framboise (raspberry brandy) or raspberry liqueur

Raspberry Sauce (optional)
14 ounces fresh raspberries (about 3¹/₂ cups), or 3 10-ounce packages frozen raspberries, thawed and drained
³/₄ cup sugar
¹/₄ cup water
Juice of 1 lemon
¹/₂ cup whipping cream
16 whole raspberries
Toasted sliced almonds (optional)

1 *For Honey-Almond parfait:* Place outer ring of 8-inch springform pan on flat serving plate; put in freezer. Whip ½ cup cream until stiff; refrigerate.

2 In top of double boiler or mixer bowl that fits snugly into a saucepan, whisk together egg, egg yolk, honey and vanilla seeds. Place over pan of boiling water and whisk vigorously until lightly thickened, 5 to 7 minutes. Remove from heat and continue beating until thick and completely cooled.

3 Fold in almonds and reserved whipped cream. Pour into chilled springform mold. Dip a finger in cold water and run around rim of mixture, forming clean edge. Return to freezer.

4 *For raspberry parfait:* Coarsely mash 14 ounces raspberries in food mill, processor or with back of large spoon. Place in saucepan with ⅓ cup sugar and bring to boil. Boil gently, stirring often, for 5 minutes. Strain to eliminate seeds. Transfer to shallow bowl and cool in freezer or refrigerator.

5 Meanwhile, whip 1 cup cream until stiff; refrigerate. Beat egg whites until they form soft peaks; then gradually add ½ cup sugar and continue to beat until stiff and shiny. Partially fold in cooled raspberry puree and framboise; add whipped cream and gently fold until blended. Pour mixture over honey-almond layer in springform mold, smoothing top with spatula. Freeze several hours or overnight.

6 *For raspberry sauce:* In saucepan, combine all sauce ingredients except lemon juice. Bring to boil, then boil gently, stirring, about 7 minutes. Reduce heat, stir in lemon juice and keep warm.

7 To garnish, remove parfait from freezer. Carefully release springform ring (if difficult, warm ring slightly with your palms). Whip ½ cup cream until stiff; form decorative border or rosettes around top and bottom edge of parfait by piping whipped cream through pastry bag fitted with star tip. Arrange 2 raspberries and 2 or 3 almond slices on top of each serving. Cut into wedges. Serve with warm raspberry sauce, if desired.

Jean-Jacques Rachou
La Côte Basque

"When I first took over La Côte Basque," Jean-Jacques Rachou confides, "there was not one restaurateur in New York who believed I was going to make it." It is not easy when you are dealing with a legend. Opened in 1958 by renowned restaurateur, the late Henri Soulé, La Côte Basque had lost its glamorous aura by the time Rachou bought it in 1979, and few believed anyone could bring it back to its former glory. Rachou brought back artist Bernard Lamotte to brighten up his original *trompe l'oeil* murals, spent a fortune renovating the kitchen and stocking the wine cellar, bought some four thousand service plates, and applied his concern for detail to every last corner of the operation. "I started doing things my own way, and I knew it would work."

Nowhere was Rachou's own way more evident than in the kitchen. The sophisticated diners of the city, who watch new restaurants with the excitement usually reserved for theater and fashion openings, were soon abuzz with the word of the man who "paints his plates." Working with multihued sauces in small plastic squeeze bottles, Rachou masks the bottom of each plate with sauce, then creates intricately traced designs in contrasting colors. Here again, some people misunderstood what he was doing, charging that he was more concerned with the appearance of his food than with its taste.

"Oh, no," he answers. "I am concerned with the taste *first*. My cooking is really very old-fashioned. Nouvelle cuisine gave us the freedom to garnish food the way we want, and I got a lot from this. But for me, there is only one cooking, and a reduction of cream with some herbs is not it."

One taste quickly dispels any doubts. Rachou builds all of his recipes—and especially his sauces—in layers, creating nuances of flavor that can only be achieved with rich stocks, multiple reductions and careful seasoning. The sauce that moistens an appetizer of escargots and wild mushrooms in feuilleté, for example, is enriched with Bordelaise sauce bound with a paste of beef marrow and flour, then strained and mounted with butter (enriched and thickened by swirling in pieces of butter bit by bit). Dishes like this cannot be achieved with shortcuts.

Many of La Côte Basque's faithful customers no longer even look at the menu, simply asking for the "special something" of the day. Rachou does not disappoint them, serving dishes such as langoustine, boned quail in pastry, studded with sweetbreads and *foie gras*, and a cassoulet from Toulouse, his birthplace.

Down a corridor from the bustling main kitchen, his trusted pastry chef Jean-Pierre Le Masson quietly prepares a praline buttercream, beating together butter, hazelnut praline paste and a light crème anglaise. A smiling, easygoing native of Normandy

Chef Jean-Jacques Rachou

who worked at Roger Vergé's three-star restaurant in France for several years, Le Masson prepares over a dozen breathtaking desserts daily, including a custard-topped apple tarte Normande, a rich chocolate cake, and the light but intensely flavored Succès aux Noisettes.

"You know," Rachou remarks thoughtfully, "I may be a businessman, but I am first an idealist. Because I treat everyone on my staff with the same care I give my customers, they give all they can. All of my energy goes into this restaurant. I am now almost fifty, and after thirty-five years of experience, I still work like I did when I was twenty. I love what I do."

Menu

Feuilleté d'Escargots et Cèpes au Santenay
Puff pastry shells filled with a ragout of snails and wild mushrooms in red wine sauce

Velouté Froid aux Herbes de Saison
Chilled cream soup with fresh herbs

Le Carré d'Agneau Roti à la Fleur de Thym
Roast rack of lamb with fresh thyme

Succès aux Noisettes
Almond meringue layers filled with hazelnut praline buttercream

Feuilleté d'Escargots et Cèpes au Santenay

4 servings

Feuilletés

- *¹/₂ pound Puff Pastry (see recipe, page 119)*
- *1 egg yolk*
- *1¹/₂ teaspoons cold water*
- *5 tablespoons unsalted butter*
- *¹/₄ cup finely chopped shallot*
- *¹/₂ pound fresh chanterelles* (about 3 to 3¹/₂ cups), coarsely chopped*
- *3 fresh cèpes, sliced*
- *24 snails (1 7¹/₂-ounce can), drained and rinsed*
- *3 tablespoons Cognac, plus more as needed*
- *³/₄ cup Santenay or other full-bodied red wine*
- *1 cup Bordelaise Sauce (see recipe, page 60) or Veal Stock (see recipe, page 118)*
- *Salt and freshly ground pepper*

Garnish

- *4 large mushrooms, stems trimmed flush with caps, caps fluted*
- *2 tablespoons water*
- *1 tablespoon fresh lemon juice*
- *1 tablespoon butter*

1   *For feuilletés*: Roll out puff pastry to large rectangle ¹/₈ inch thick. Use 5-inch oval or 4-inch round cutter to cut 4 pieces of pastry. Place them on baking sheet. Stir together egg yolk and water; lightly brush pastry with this egg wash. Chill pastry 30 minutes.

2   Preheat oven to 400°F. Bake feuilletés 20 minutes, then lower heat to 350°F and continue baking until golden brown, 5 to 10 minutes longer. Cool on rack.

3   In saucepan, heat 3 tablespoons butter over medium-high heat; add shallot and stir until wilted, about 2 minutes. Add chanterelles and cèpes and stir until quite dry, 6 to 8 minutes. Add snails and toss 1 minute. Add 3 tablespoons Cognac, light carefully with match, and cook 1 to 2 minutes. Transfer this mixture to sieve placed over bowl and return pan to heat. Add red wine and reduce by half, scraping up any browned bits in pan, about 4 minutes. Add Bordelaise Sauce or Veal Stock and reduce until thickened enough to coat a spoon lightly, 3 to 5 minutes. Remove pan from heat, swirl in remaining butter a little at a time, and adjust seasoning to taste with salt and pepper and a few drops of Cognac.

4   *For garnish*: Slice tops off feuilletés and scoop out insides. Return feuilletés and their lids to oven briefly to reheat. In small saucepan, combine mushrooms, water, lemon juice and 1 tablespoon butter. Bring

*Other wild or cultivated mushrooms may be substituted.

Jean-Jacques Rachou uses plastic squeeze bottles and a knife tip to "paint" his serving plates with sauces

to a boil over medium-high heat; cover and cook, shaking pan occasionally, until just tender, about 4 minutes. Remove mushrooms; drain and cut into thick slices.

5   To assemble, add snail-mushroom mixture to sauce and bring to simmer. Place heated pastry shells on 4 heated plates and fill with snail mixture. Garnish with mushroom slices by overlapping them along 1 edge of each shell. Spoon any remaining sauce over, replace lids at a slight angle, and serve immediately.

Makes about 3 cups

Bordelaise Sauce

2 tablespoons (¹/₄ stick) unsalted butter
8 medium shallots, roughly chopped
1 garlic clove, roughly chopped
Bouquet garni (leek, parsley, thyme, and bay leaf tied together in a cheesecloth bag)
1 bottle (750 ml) dry red wine
3 ounces fresh veal marrow or beef marrow
2 tablespoons all purpose flour
3 cups Veal Stock (see recipe, page 118)

1 Heat butter in medium saucepan; add shallots and garlic and cook until soft, about 5 minutes. Add bouquet garni and wine; bring to boil.

2 Meanwhile, in mixing bowl, mash together marrow and flour with fork until nearly smooth. Whisk into wine mixture and boil gently, whisking occasionally, until reduced by half. Add Veal Stock and simmer gently until thickened enough to coat a spoon lightly.

Velouté Froid aux Herbes de Saison

4 servings

2 tablespoons (¼ stick)
   unsalted butter
1 cup finely shredded sorrel
   leaves
¼ cup shredded fresh basil
   leaves
2 tablespoons chopped fresh
   chives
2 tablespoons chopped fresh
   tarragon

2 cups Chicken stock (see
   recipe, page 118)
   Salt and freshly ground
   white pepper
6 egg yolks
2 cups whipping cream
   Fresh lemon juice
   Crème fraîche or sour cream
   (optional garnish)

1 Heat butter in saucepan; add sorrel. Stir over medium heat until wilted, 2 to 3 minutes. Add basil, chives and tarragon and stir 2 minutes. Add stock; bring to boil and boil 5 minutes. Season to taste with salt and white pepper.

2 In mixing bowl, whisk together egg yolks and cream. Very gradually whisk hot mixture into cream mixture. Return to saucepan and stir constantly over low heat until lightly thickened, about 4 minutes. *Do not boil.*

3 Transfer soup to bowl set in larger bowl of ice water and stir until cool. Refrigerate. Add fresh lemon juice to taste; adjust seasoning with salt and white pepper. Garnish with crème fraîche or sour cream.

Le Carré d'Agneau Roti à la Fleur de Thym

Accompany this rack of lamb with a selection of vegetables of your choice, such as souffléed potatoes, lightly sautéed cherry tomato halves, carrots, zucchini or asparagus tips.

4 servings

2 racks of lamb (about 2 pounds each), Frenched (reserve blade bones and trimmings for Lamb Stock)
Salt and freshly ground pepper
2 tablespoons chopped fresh thyme or 1½ teaspoons dried
1 tablespoon vegetable oil
1 medium onion, coarsely chopped

1 carrot, coarsely chopped
1 celery stalk, coarsely chopped
1 teaspoon chopped fresh rosemary or ½ teaspoon dried
1 cup dry white wine
2 cups Lamb Stock (see following recipe) or Veal Stock (see recipe, page 118)
Watercress sprigs (garnish)

1 Preheat oven to 450°F. Trim lamb, leaving about ¼ inch fat, and score fat in crisscross pattern. Wrap exposed bone ends with aluminum foil. Season both sides with salt and pepper; rub in half of thyme.

2 Heat oil in large heavy ovenproof skillet over medium-high heat. Add lamb, fat side down. Sauté, shaking pan occasionally, until lightly golden, about 2 minutes. Turn and lightly brown other side. Turn again, fat side down.

3 Place skillet in oven and lower heat to 400°F. Roast 10 minutes. Remove racks and set aside; pour off excess fat. Add onion, carrot, celery, remaining thyme and rosemary to skillet and return racks to pan, fat side up. Roast 12 to 15 minutes longer for medium rare, then transfer racks to work surface and place skillet over medium-high heat.

4 Add white wine to skillet and reduce slightly, scraping up any browned bits in pan. Add stock and cook until very lightly thickened, about 15 minutes. Carve lamb into individual chops and arrange on heated serving plates. Strain stock mixture; degrease and season to taste with salt and pepper. Pour sauce over lamb, garnish with watercress sprigs and serve immediately.

Le Carré d'Agneau Roti à la Fleur de Thym

Makes 4 to 6 cups

Lamb Stock

*Bones and trimmings from
2 racks of lamb*
*¹/₂ cup water, plus more as
needed*
*1 cup chopped fresh or canned
tomatoes*
1 medium onion, chopped
2 carrots, chopped

*2 celery stalks, trimmed and
chopped*
5 garlic cloves, chopped
*1 sprig fresh thyme or ¹/₂
teaspoon dried*
2 bay leaves
6 black peppercorns

1   Preheat oven to 400°F. In roasting pan, roast bones and trimmings until well browned, about 45 minutes, stirring occasionally.

2   Transfer bones and trimmings to stockpot; degrease roasting pan. Place over medium-high heat and stir in ¹/₂ cup water, scraping up any browned bits. Pour these deglazed juices into stockpot. Add remaining ingredients and water to cover. Bring to simmer over medium heat, reduce heat to low, cover partially, and simmer 3 to 4 hours, skimming frequently. Strain stock into bowl through colander lined with double layer of dampened cheesecloth. Gently press solids to extract all liquid; discard solids. Cool; remove fat from surface.

Succès aux Noisettes

10 to 12 servings

Almond Meringue Layers
   6 egg whites, room
      temperature
   2¹/₂ tablespoons sugar
   2¹/₂ cups sifted powdered sugar,
      plus more as needed
   ³/₄ cup ground blanched
      almonds (about 2 ounces)

Hazelnut Praline Buttercream
   1 cup milk
   4 egg yolks
   ¹/₃ cup plus 1 tablespoon sugar
   1 cup (2 sticks) unsalted
      butter, room temperature
   4 ounces hazelnut praline
      paste*
   1¹/₃ cups toasted sliced almonds
      (about 4 ounces) (toast 7 to
      10 minutes at 350°F)

1　*For almond meringue layers*: Preheat oven to 325°F. Cut out three 10-inch parchment paper circles and one 10-inch cardboard circle. Set parchment circles on baking sheets.

2　Beat egg whites to soft peaks; gradually add 2¹/₂ tablespoons sugar and continue beating until stiff. Combine 2¹/₂ cups powdered sugar and ground almonds; fold into egg whites.

3　Spoon mixture into pastry bag fitted with a no. 6 round tip. Pipe meringue onto parchment circles, starting in center and spiraling outward just to edge. Dust lightly with powdered sugar. Bake until crisp and very lightly golden, 25 to 30 minutes. Cool on racks.

4　*For buttercream*: Place medium bowl in large bowl of ice water; set aside. Bring milk to boiling point in heavy saucepan over medium heat. Meanwhile, beat egg yolks in large mixer bowl until smooth. Gradually add ¹/₃ cup plus 1 tablespoon sugar and continue beating until mixture is pale yellow and forms a ribbon when beaters are lifted, about 7 minutes. Gradually add boiling milk to yolk mixture, beating constantly. Return to saucepan; cook over low heat, stirring with wooden spoon, for 30 seconds. Immediately pour custard into bowl set over ice water. Cool, stirring occasionally.

Available at specialty stores or by mail order from H. Roth & Sons, 1577 First Ave., New York, NY 10028; (212) 734-1110.

Using a parchment paper circle as a guide, almond meringue is piped in a spiral to make a layer of the Succès aux Noisettes

Succès aux Noisettes

5 Beat butter and praline paste in large bowl until smooth and creamy. Gradually beat in cooled custard.

6 To assemble, using cardboard as a guide, trim meringues to even circles. Carefully peel off parchment paper. Choose 1 meringue with a smooth bottom and set aside.

7 Spread ¹/₃ of the cream onto 1 meringue layer. Top with second meringue, centering it over bottom layer; smooth on another layer of buttercream. Top with remaining meringue, smooth side up, pressing gently. Frost sides and top of cake with remaining buttercream. Gently press sliced almonds onto sides and top with spatula.

8 Dust about 2 inches of rim and 2-inch circle in center with powdered sugar. Transfer to serving platter. Let stand at room temperature 30 minutes before serving in wedges.

Seppi Renggli
The Four Seasons

Chef Seppi Renggli with co-owners Tom Margittai (left) and Paul Kovi

The Four Seasons perfectly captures New York's electric energy. Designed by Philip Johnson in Mies van der Rohe's Seagram Building, it is a restaurant on a grand scale. Through a dramatic corridor, you are escorted past Picasso's stage curtain for *Le Tricorne*, past the glass-enclosed day wine cellar, to arrive in the Pool Room, where tables surround a burbling pool of Carrara marble and potted trees that change with the seasons. The entire effect, down to the gleaming silver bread baskets, is one of luxurious calm.

From its opening twenty-five years ago, The Four Seasons has been devoted to serving the best American products prepared in a striking style that synthesizes native ingredients with Old World techniques. Today, this sort of imaginative approach to cooking is known as the New American Cuisine; when it was first devised at The Four Seasons, it was revolutionary. Since Hungarian-born owners Tom Margittai and Paul Kovi took over in 1973 the restaurant has reached even greater culinary heights.

Chef Josef (Seppi) Renggli, a lively Swiss-born master, at fifty, is in his prime. One of the world's most tirelessly inventive chefs, Renggli has an exuberant sense of seasoning, quickly grinding together sea salt, peppercorns and a small chili to add punch to his salmon rillettes (his inspired version of the French classic usually made with pork or goose). He liberally infuses classic as well as new dishes with jalapeño peppers, fresh ginger and curry spices from the East (his wife is Indonesian), plus a profusion of fresh herbs.

He uses the best native products in a deft style that is never self-consciously "creative." For example, his remarkable polenta with Gorgonzola is half Italian polenta, half American spoon-bread. And his plates are beautiful compositions in vibrant colors: Crisp golden quail is offset by glazed polenta and Kitchen Chef Christian (Hitch) Albin's cranberry relish—all placed on oversize white plates in a clean, modern style.

"Hey, Hitch," Renggli calls, grinning as he begins cutting up vegetables for his winter soup, "toss me some turnips!" It is clear that these two Swiss (both of whom work in clogs) have worked together for a long time. With a kitchen brigade of forty-two, including pastry chefs, they prepare seven to eight hundred meals every day, introducing a new seasonal menu every four to six weeks.

When spring arrives, Renggli roasts baby lamb and goat and prepares salmon and asparagus differently every day. In summer, "Everything with tomatoes!," he declares. There is cool tomato bisque served with a scoop of basil sorbet; fresh pasta with tomatoes several ways; and a whole tomato baked with a pungent stuffing of basil and mozzarella.

When the temperature goes down, Renggli tops pasta with a buttery toss of fragrant wild mushrooms and offers a variety of game specialties, including quail with juniper, wild boar, breast of pheasant with red currant sauce and polenta, and a whole loin of venison roasted in a salt crust.

One of the restaurant's signature desserts is a chocolate cake created by Italian-born master pastry chef Bruno Comin. "The cake layers will fall a little after they bake—don't worry, that's okay," Comin says. "But anyone can make this cake at home. I know because I got a photograph of it from a lady in Vermont who did it perfectly! That made me very happy."

Menu

Salmon Rillettes
Appetizer spread of poached fresh salmon, smoked salmon, and salmon roe

Winter Vegetable Potage
Puree of seasonal vegetables, served in an acorn squash

Roast Quail with Juniper Berries, Served with Gorgonzola Polenta and Cranberry Relish

Bruno's Chocolate Cake
Chocolate-almond sponge cake layers with chocolate whipped cream, surrounded by strips of dark and white chocolate

Salmon Rillettes

8 servings

Court Bouillon

2¹/₂ cups cold water
1 medium onion, sliced
1 carrot, sliced
1 celery stalk, sliced
1 leek (white part only),
    trimmed and sliced
    (optional)
3 fennel stalks (optional)
1 sprig fresh thyme or pinch of
    dried
    Few stems fresh dill
¹/₂ teaspoon salt
4 white peppercorns

³/₄ pound fresh salmon fillets
    or steaks (leave skin on),
    trimmed

1 tablespoon sea salt
¹/₂ teaspoon whole peppercorns
1 small dried chili
1 cup (2 sticks) unsalted
    butter, softened slightly
1 tablespoon Armagnac
³/₄ pound smoked salmon,
    trimmed and cut into shreds
4 ounces salmon roe

Toast Strips

Olive oil
1 loaf good-quality white
    bread, crusts trimmed, sliced
    ³/₄ inch thick, each slice cut
    into 3 long strips

1   *For court bouillon*: Place water, onion, carrot, celery, leek, fennel, thyme, dill, salt and 4 peppercorns in saucepan and bring to boil. Cover and simmer 25 minutes. Strain and reserve liquid.

2   Bring strained liquid to boil in skillet. Add salmon and lower heat to simmer. Place sheet of buttered parchment paper or aluminum foil, buttered side down, over salmon. Poach until just opaque in center, about 8 minutes, or about 10 minutes per inch of thickness; *do not overcook*. Remove from heat and cool salmon completely in broth.

3   Use small spice or coffee mill to grind sea salt, ¹/₂ teaspoon peppercorns, and chili.

4   Drain poached salmon, remove skin and cut into ¹/₂-inch pieces. Place salmon pieces, butter, Armagnac and pinch of the seasoning mixture into processor and blend into very smooth puree. Add shredded smoked salmon to processor and process with rapid on and off turns just until mixture is blended. There should still be visible shreds of smoked salmon. Transfer to mixing bowl.

5   Gently fold salmon roe into mixture until blended, taking care not to crush eggs. Adjust seasoning. Spoon mixture into 4-cup soufflé dish, straight-sided gratin dish, or casserole, lightly tapping mold on towel-lined surface to eliminate air bubbles. Cover with plastic wrap and chill. (Can be prepared 1 or 2 days ahead.)

6　*For toast strips*: Preheat oven to 325°F. Rub baking sheet with thin film of olive oil. Arrange bread strips on baking sheet and bake on center rack of oven, without turning, until lightly golden, 15 to 20 minutes.

7　Remove rillettes from refrigerator 20 minutes before serving. Dip serving spoon in cold water and scoop onto cool plates. Serve with warm toast strips.

Winter Vegetable Potage

At Thanksgiving dinner at The Four Seasons, this soup is served in a hollowed-out acorn squash. To serve it that way, slice off the tops and a thin sliver from the bottom of the acorn squash, then hollow out the insides. Pour in the finished soup and bake on a baking sheet, uncovered, at 375°F until the squash is tender, about 30 minutes. The squash will be tender enough to be scraped from the shell and eaten with the soup. The vegetables in this soup can be varied according to what is in season, as long as you maintain the proportion of solids to liquid.

12 to 16 servings

$^1/_2$ cup (1 stick) unsalted butter
1 medium onion, coarsely chopped
1 leek, trimmed, split lengthwise and coarsely chopped
3 celery stalks, coarsely chopped
3 garlic cloves, crushed and coarsely chopped
1 small fresh jalapeño chili, split lengthwise, seeded and chopped
2 large carrots, peeled and coarsely chopped
$^1/_2$ medium head savoy cabbage, cored and coarsely chopped
2 medium baking potatoes, peeled and coarsely chopped
2 medium white turnips, peeled and coarsely chopped
1 medium fennel bulb, coarsely chopped
1 medium kohlrabi, peeled and coarsely chopped (optional)
1 medium celery root (celeriac), pared and coarsely chopped
2 to 3 stalks broccoli, coarsely cut up
10 to 12 sprigs Italian flat-leaf parsley
10 cups Chicken Stock (about), (see recipe, page 118)
3 cups whipping cream
Salt and freshly ground pepper
Sour cream (garnish)
Chopped fresh chives (garnish)

1　In large saucepan or casserole, heat butter over medium-low heat. Add onion, leek, celery, garlic and jalapeño chili. Cook, covered, 30 minutes, stirring occasionally.

2　Add carrots, cabbage, potatoes, turnips, fennel, kohlrabi, celery root, broccoli, parsley, and enough stock to nearly cover. Bring to boil; lower heat and simmer, uncovered, 30 minutes, or until very tender.

3　Puree soup, working in batches as needed, in processor or blender. Rinse out pan, pour in soup and bring to simmer. Add cream and salt and pepper to taste; return to simmer. Serve with garnish of sour cream and chives.

Roast Quail with Juniper Berries, Served with Gorgonzola Polenta and Cranberry Relish

6 servings

12 quail, necks and feet
   removed
 6 thin slices pancetta (Italian
   dry-cured unsmoked bacon)
   or bacon, coarsely chopped
12 fresh sage leaves or ¹/₂
   teaspoon dried
36 juniper berries, toasted in
   dry skillet 5 minutes

Salt and freshly ground
   pepper
¹/₄ cup olive oil
¹/₄ cup gin
¹/₂ cup dry white wine
 2 cups Veal Stock (see recipe,
   p. 118)

1 Preheat oven to 450°F. Holding quail, breast up, tuck wing tips under. Place a little of pancetta, a sage leaf, and 2 juniper berries in cavity of each bird. Sprinkle cavity and outside of each bird with a little salt and pepper. Push each leg joint downward and fasten it to carcass with toothpick, pushing 1 toothpick through both legs.

2 Heat olive oil in heavy large skillet over very high heat. Arrange birds in pan, breasts down. Sauté, shaking pan occasionally until breasts are lightly golden, 2 to 3 minutes. Place skillet in oven and roast 5 to 6 minutes. Use tongs to turn birds' breasts up and continue to roast until golden brown, about 6 minutes. Remove skillet from oven, transfer birds to 6 warm serving plates; keep warm while preparing sauce.

3 Discard fat from skillet and place pan over medium-high heat. Add gin and wine, scraping up any browned bits in pan. Add stock and boil gently until reduced enough to coat a spoon lightly. Stir in remaining juniper berries; adjust seasoning. Pour over birds and serve.

6 servings

Gorgonzola Polenta

 3 cups milk
 3 tablespoons unsalted butter
³/₄ cup cornmeal (not stone-
   ground)
 3 tablespoons sour cream
2¹/₂ tablespoons grated Gruyère
   cheese
2¹/₂ tablespoons freshly grated
   Parmesan cheese

¹/₃ cup crumbled Gorgonzola
   cheese, plus 6 thin 1-inch-
   square slices
¹/₃ cup golden raisins
   Freshly grated nutmeg
   Salt and freshly ground
   pepper
   Fine breadcrumbs

1 In heavy-bottomed saucepan, bring milk and butter to boil. Add cornmeal in thin stream, whisking constantly. When mixture becomes very thick, continue to boil while stirring constantly with wooden spoon, until very thick and smooth, about 5 minutes.

2 Stir in sour cream, grated Gruyère, Parmesan, crumbled Gorgonzola, raisins and a little nutmeg, beating until smooth. Remove from heat; add salt and pepper to taste.

3 Spoon cornmeal mixture into 6 ½-cup ramekins or custard cups, tapping molds gently on work surface to settle mixture, and smoothing tops with spatula. Cool at least 15 minutes.

4 Use a knife to loosen polenta from ramekins and unmold onto generously buttered baking dish. Place slice of Gorgonzola on top of each; sprinkle with fine layer of breadcrumbs. Bake in 450°F oven (along with quail, if desired) for 10 to 12 minutes, then broil just until lightly golden. Serve immediately.

Roast Quail with Juniper Berries, Served with Gorgonzola Polenta and Cranberry Relish

Unusual and delicious, this recipe is from The Four Seasons's Kitchen Chef Christian (Hitch) Albin.

Makes about 6 cups

Cranberry Relish

1 large navel orange
1 lime
1 tablespoon grated fresh ginger
2 cinnamon sticks
1 dried chili

1 vanilla bean, split lengthwise
2 cups sugar
1 cup raisins
2 pounds fresh cranberries

1   Cut orange and lime, with their skins, into ¼-inch dice. Set aside. Tie ginger, cinnamon sticks, chili and vanilla bean in cheesecloth and set aside.

2   Place sugar in heavy large skillet, preferably one with straight sides. Stir constantly over high heat until sugar turns light amber. Sugar must be cooked carefully to prevent burning; break up lumps as you go. (If there are still lumps of sugar after it begins to color, work over low heat, or off heat, until mixture is smooth.)

3   Stir in orange, lime and bag of spices, and cook over high heat, stirring constantly, 5 minutes. Fold in raisins and cranberries, stirring gently to coat with caramelized sugar. Cook over medium heat, stirring gently, until about half of cranberries pop open, about 10 minutes. Remove pan from heat and cool.

4   Remove bag of spices and spoon relish into sterilized jars. Cover tightly and refrigerate 1 month. This relish keeps about 3 months.

Bruno's Chocolate Cake

12 servings

Cake

9 eggs, separated, room temperature
1 tablespoon dark rum
¼ teaspoon vanilla extract
¼ teaspoon cream of tartar
8 tablespoons sugar
12 ounces semisweet chocolate, melted

6 tablespoons (¾ stick) unsalted butter, melted
3 tablespoons cornstarch
2 tablespoons unsweetened cocoa
2½ ounces amaretti (about 10 Italian macaroons), finely ground

Chocolate Cream

4 ounces semisweet chocolate, melted
1/2 cup hot water
2 cups whipping cream
2 tablespoons dark rum

3 ounces semisweet chocolate, melted

3 ounces white chocolate, melted
Unsweetened cocoa
Chocolate leaves* (optional garnish)

1 *For cake*: Preheat oven to 375°F. Butter and flour 3 9-inch round cake pans.

2 Beat yolks until they are pale yellow and form a ribbon when beaters are lifted, about 5 minutes. Beat in rum and vanilla.

*For chocolate leaves, brush melted chocolate on undersides of holly or lemon leaves; refrigerate until firm; carefully peel off leaves.

Bruno's Chocolate Cake

Pastry chef Bruno Comin decorates his special chocolate cake with strips of dark and white chocolate

3   Beat whites with cream of tartar to soft peaks. Add sugar 1 tablespoon at a time and continue beating until stiff and shiny.

4   Stir 12 ounce semisweet chocolate and butter into yolks until well combined. Gently fold in ¼ of egg whites to lighten batter, then gently fold in remaining whites.

5   Sift together cornstarch and cocoa; combine with ground amaretti. Gently fold into batter.

6   Divide batter among prepared pans. Bake until centers of cakes rise and tops begin to crack, 18 to 20 minutes. Cool 10 minutes in pans, then cool completely on wire rack (cakes will fall slightly).

7   *For chocolate cream*: Whisk together 4 ounces semisweet chocolate and hot water; cool to room temperature. Whip cream until nearly stiff. Gently fold chocolate mixture and rum into whipped cream.

8   To assemble, set aside ¼ of chocolate cream for decorating top of cake. Spread remainder evenly between 3 layers, stacking them neatly, then spread over top and sides.

9   Measure height of cake. On sheet of parchment or waxed paper, spread 3 ounces melted semisweet chocolate into rectangle ¹⁄₁₆-inch-thick and as wide as the cake is high. Repeat with melted white chocolate on another sheet of parchment. Refrigerate until chocolate is firm but not brittle, about 15 minutes. Cut chocolate crosswise into ¾-inch-wide strips. Refrigerate to refirm chocolate, about 15 minutes.

10   Carefully arrange strips alternately around edges of cake, gently pressing into icing. Spoon reserved chocolate cream into pastry bag fitted with a no. 3 round tip. Pipe mixture in straight lines atop cake. Dust lightly with cocoa; refrigerate. Garnish with chocolate leaves. Bring to room temperature before serving.

Leslie Revsin
One Fifth Avenue

Much is made of the fact that in 1972 Leslie Revsin was the first woman ever to cook in the kitchen of the Waldorf-Astoria Hotel. But Leslie's large and faithful clientele responds to her cooking not because she is a woman but because she is a first-rate chef.

She started cooking at a time when the phenomenon of the young American chef forging his or her own style had not yet made its way to every corner of the land. Trained in the hotel and restaurant management program at New York City Community College (now New York City Technical College), she first attracted notice at P.S. 77, and soon thereafter opened her own place in Greenwich Village. Restaurant Leslie was almost too good to be true: a cozy atmosphere, a limited menu, bring-your-own wine, and distinctive food.

Revsin recently took over the kitchens at One Fifth Avenue, a large restaurant decorated in Art Deco glamor with many fittings from the cruise ship *Coronia*. Here she cooks the way she always has, rarely calling attention to the chef's technique but, rather, seeking to highlight the flavors of the ingredients themselves. In dishes such as pan-roasted rabbit, for example, the emphasis is on heightening the rabbit's own flavor: careful browning in olive oil to create a rich glaze in the pan; deglazing the crusty bits with white wine to release the flavor into the braising liquid; slow oven braising to keep the meat moist. The finished dish is served with a bright mix of coarsely pureed beets and a toss of spinach and beet greens. This is masterful composition of tastes, textures and colors.

Revsin's cooking ranges from simple bistro fare to delicate dishes, such as a buttery *blanquette* of fish, yet it is always marked by inventive combinations. Her Roquefort beignets, with their remarkable play of taste, texture and temperature contrasts, are not conventional beignets (fritters), but cheese-stuffed crepes that are dipped in a light batter and fried crisp. Another such dish is an unexpected but successful pairing of sweetbreads with caviar. Her food is uncluttered and without artifice.

While Revsin has, by her example, opened the way for women chefs in this country, she takes a much broader view: "Great cooks," she believes, "are genderless. They must have both feminine and masculine components. A great cook can express the entire range of human capacity and feeling.

"I get impatient," she explains, "with cooking that is so refined that the food has no real depth of flavor, and with food that is overcomplicated with multiple components and garnishes. What I am interested in is real food. After all, with food, the point is pleasure."

Chef Leslie Revsin

Menu

Roquefort Beignets with Apple Puree

Fish Broth with Oysters and Saffron

A rich broth with seafood, cellophane noodles, and radicchio

Pan-roasted Rabbit with Fresh Herbs

Marinated rabbit pieces with white wine and sweet garlic cloves,
served with roast beet puree and spinach and beet greens

Fresh Pineapple with Rum Cream

Roquefort Beignets with Apple Puree

Makes 1 dozen

Crepe Batter
- 2 eggs
- 1/2 cup milk
- 1/2 cup water, or more
- 1 cup sifted all purpose flour
  Salt and freshly ground
  white pepper
- 2 tablespoons Clarified Butter
  (see recipe, page 120)
  Olive oil

Fritter Batter
- 1/4 cup all purpose flour
- 2 tablespoons cornstarch
- 1 teaspoon baking powder
- 1/2 teaspoon salt
- 1 egg
- 1/4 cup water, or more
- 1/2 teaspoon vegetable oil

Apple Puree
- 4 tart apples, such as Granny
  Smith, peeled, cored and cut
  into 8 wedges
  Water

Filling
- 4 ounces Roquefort cheese,
  crumbled (about 1 cup),
  room temperature
- 1 1/2 teaspoons egg yolk

  Vegetable oil (for deep
  frying)

1 *For Crepes*: Combine eggs, milk and ¹/₂ cup water. Gradually add 1 cup flour, whisking until smooth; whisk in salt and pepper and Clarified Butter. Thin with water, if necessary, to consistency of whipping cream. Cover and refrigerate several hours or overnight.

2 If crepe batter has thickened, thin with water to consistency of whipping cream. Brush 7-inch skillet (preferably non stick) with thin film of olive oil. Place over medium-high heat. When hot, add about 3 tablespoons of crepe batter and swirl to coat pan. Cook until lightly golden, about 1 minute; then turn and cook second side 30 seconds. Continue with remaining batter, stacking crepes between waxed paper.

3 *For fritter batter*: Sift ¹/₄ cup flour, cornstarch, baking powder and salt into mixing bowl. In second bowl, combine egg, ¹/₄ cup water and vegetable oil; gradually stir into flour just until smooth; *do not overmix*. Refrigerate, covered.

4 *For apple puree*: Place apples in heavy saucepan over medium-low heat, adding a few drops of water if they are dry. Cover pan and cook, stirring occasionally, until slightly softened, 10 to 15 minutes. Break up into 1-inch pieces. Refrigerate, covered, until cold.

5 *For filling*: Blend Roquefort and egg yolk (mixture will be lumpy). Cut off any dry edges from crepes, squaring them slightly. Place rounded teaspoonful of cheese mixture in center of spotty side of a crepe, mounding it slightly. Fold crepe into thirds horizontally (as you would a letter), then fold sides in so that they overlap slightly, forming neat package about 2 inches square. Place folded side down on tray lined with waxed paper; repeat with remaining crepes and filling. Cover folded crepes with damp cloth, then with plastic wrap, then with aluminum foil. Chill several hours or overnight.

6 In large skillet or saucepan, place 2 inches vegetable oil and heat to 375°F (when a small piece of bread dropped into oil sizzles steadily). Thin fritter batter with water, if necessary, so that it flows from a spoon but is not watery. Use 2 forks to dip folded crepes into fritter batter; then lift out, draining off excess, and transfer to hot oil (*do not crowd*). Fry until golden, turning once, 1¹/₂ to 2 minutes. Drain on paper towels and serve with apple puree.

Leslie Revsin tests the consistency of the crepe batter for her Roquefort Beignets

Fish Broth with Oysters and Saffron

4 servings

*¹/₄ cup (¹/₂ stick) unsalted
butter*
*1 medium onion, coarsely
chopped*
*1¹/₂ carrots, peeled, halved
lengthwise and sliced ¹/₂
inch thick*
*3 celery stalks, trimmed,
halved lengthwise and sliced
¹/₂ inch thick*
*2 small leeks, halved
lengthwise, and sliced ¹/₂
inch thick*
6 parsley stems
*2 cloves garlic, crushed and
peeled*
2 bay leaves

¹/₂ teaspoon juniper berries
*1 large ripe tomato, cut into
wedges*
*2 to 3 pounds fish bones and
trimmings*
1 cup dry white wine
6 cups cold water (about)
¹/₄ teaspoon salt, or to taste
4 clams
8 oysters, shucked
*1 ounce mung bean threads
(cellophane noodles),
soaked in hot water 20
minutes, drained and cut
into 2-inch lengths*
8 radicchio leaves
¹/₄ teaspoon saffron threads

1   Melt butter in stockpot over medium-high heat. Add onion, carrots, celery, leeks, parsley, garlic, bay leaves and juniper berries, tossing to coat with butter. When vegetables begin to sizzle, reduce heat to medium low and cover. Cook, covered, stirring occasionally, about 10 minutes.

2   Add tomato and stir 1 minute. Add fish bones and trimmings and white wine; cook 5 minutes, stirring occasionally. Add cold water to cover and raise heat to medium high. Bring to boil, skimming all froth from surface. Immediately lower heat and simmer gently, uncovered, 35 to 40 minutes. Strain, pressing solids firmly to extract all liquid (discard solids). Add salt to taste.

3   Heat 4 cups fish broth in saucepan. Steam clams separately in small amount of broth just until shells open, removing each shell as it opens. Transfer to 4 warm soup bowls; strain clam broth into warm fish broth, avoiding any grit at the bottom.

4   Add oysters to fish broth and cook gently over low heat, uncovered, just until edges curl, about 1 minute. Place 2 oysters in each bowl. Ladle warm broth into bowls and add 2 tablespoons mung bean threads. Add radicchio leaves and saffron and serve.

Pan-roasted Rabbit with Fresh Herbs

Leslie Revsin uses brown chicken stock in this recipe. To prepare it, roast chicken bones in 450°F oven 30 minutes, then add vegetables (see recipe for Chicken Stock, page 118) and roast 15 minutes longer. Transfer to stockpot. Pour off fat from roasting pan, deglaze with water, add deglazing liquid to stockpot with fresh water, and proceed as for regular Chicken Stock.

4 servings

1 3- to 4-pound rabbit

Marinade

¹/₃ cup brandy
¹/₄ cup dry red wine
2 tablespoons extra-virgin olive oil
4 garlic cloves, peeled and crushed
2 sprigs fresh thyme, or ¹/₂ teaspoon dried
3 sprigs winter savory, or ¹/₂ teaspoon dried
2 sprigs fresh rosemary, or ¹/₄ teaspoon dried
2 sprigs fresh marjoram or ¹/₄ teaspoon dried
1 teaspoon fresh oregano or ¹/₂ teaspoon dried
5 bay leaves, crumbled

3 tablespoons juniper berries, crushed
¹/₂ cup extra-virgin olive oil (about)
Salt and freshly ground pepper
1 cup dry white wine
2 cups Chicken Stock or more (see recipe, page 118)
8 garlic cloves, peeled
1 tablespoon extra-virgin olive oil
³/₄ teaspoon arrowroot or cornstarch
1 tablespoon cold water
1¹/₂ tablespoons brandy
Roast Beet Puree (see following recipe)
Spinach and beet greens*

1   To marinate: Ask butcher to cut up rabbit as follows: forelegs left whole, hind legs cut into 3 pieces each (lower joint; thigh cut diagonally into 2 pieces), rib section cut into 3 pieces, loin cut into 3 pieces, neck left whole. At least 2 days before serving, place rabbit in shallow glass or enamel pan and add marinade ingredients. Turn rabbit pieces over to coat. Marinate, covered, in refrigerator, turning occasionally.

2   Preheat oven to 325°F. Remove rabbit from marinade. In a heavy large skillet, heat about ¹/₄ cup olive oil over medium-high heat; add half of rabbit pieces and sprinkle with salt and pepper. Sauté, turning pieces once, until golden brown, about 5 minutes. Transfer to ovenproof casserole. Discard fat from skillet and add ¹/₂ cup white wine, scraping up all browned bits in pan. Boil 2 minutes and add to casserole. Repeat procedure, browning remaining rabbit, deglazing and adding rabbit and liquid to casserole.

3   Bring Chicken Stock to boil; skim and pour into casserole (liquid should not quite cover meat). Place casserole, partially covered, in lower third of the oven. After 50 minutes, check forelegs, racks and loins. If they are tender, remove. Continue cooking until remaining

Blanch 1¹/₂ pounds fresh spinach, stems removed, and reserved greens from 4 beets. Drain, rinse under cold water and squeeze out all liquid. Toss greens in skillet over medium-high heat with 2 tablespoons butter until heated through. Season with salt.

pieces are tender, 1 to 1½ hours total cooking time (timing can vary depending on size and tenderness of rabbit). Transfer to serving plates and keep warm.

4   Meanwhile, blanch garlic in boiling salted water for 30 seconds; drain. Blanch again for 30 seconds; drain. Place in small skillet with 1 tablespoon olive oil; sauté over high heat 1 minute. Place skillet in oven until garlic is golden, 25 to 30 minutes. Cut each clove into 3 or 4 pieces; set aside.

5   When rabbit is tender, place skillet with cooking liquid over high heat and boil until reduced by half, about 15 minutes. Skim all fat from surface. In small cup, stir together arrowroot and water; whisk into reduced cooking liquid and return to boil. Add brandy, adjust seasoning with salt and pepper, and skim if necessary. Stir in reserved garlic pieces and pour over rabbit. Serve with Roast Beet Puree and spinach and beet greens.

4 servings

Roast Beet Puree

4 medium beets with greens, stems trimmed (reserve greens)	*4 bay leaves*
	10 peppercorns
½ teaspoon dried oregano	*2 tablespoons extra-virgin olive oil*
½ teaspoon dried thyme	*2 tablespoons (¼ stick) unsalted butter, cut into pieces*
¼ teaspoon fennel seed	
¼ teaspoon ground coriander	
¼ teaspoon dried rosemary	*Salt*

1   Preheat oven to 450°F. Place beets in roasting pan; sprinkle with next 7 ingredients, drizzle with olive oil and stir to coat. Bake, uncovered, until tender when pierced with fork, about 1 hour. When cool enough to handle, slip off skins.

2   Quarter beets and transfer to processor. Process until coarsely chopped. Transfer to small saucepan and stir over medium heat until heated through. Add butter and stir until glossy. Season to taste with salt; serve immediately.

Fresh Pineapple with Rum Cream

4 servings

Rum Cream

3 egg yolks	*½ cup (1 stick) unsalted butter, chilled and cut into pieces*
3 tablespoons sugar (preferably superfine)	
	2 tablespoons dark rum

Pan-roasted Rabbit with Fresh Herbs

¹/4 *cup whipping cream*
1 *ripe medium-large*
pineapple

8 *very thin slices ripe*
cantaloupe (garnish)

1 *For Rum Cream*: In top of double boiler, blend egg yolks and sugar. Place over boiling water and whisk until warm to the touch. Add butter, 1 or 2 pieces at a time. When all butter has been incorporated, whisk until lightly thickened, 1 or 2 minutes longer. Remove from heat and cool, whisking occasionally. When cool, gradually whisk in rum; fold in about ¹/3 cup whipped cream. Reserve remaining whipped cream for another use.

2 Cut off base and stem of pineapple, reserving a few small leaves for garnish. Quarter lengthwise, then remove skin and core with sharp knife. Slice each quarter lengthwise into ¹/4-inch-thick slices.

3 Arrange pineapple slices on chilled plates, overlapping slightly. Gently curl cantaloupe slices in the shape of an *S* and place 2 pieces on each plate as garnish. Garnish with reserved pineapple leaves. Spoon some rum cream over pineapple; serve remainder separately.

Felipe Rojas-Lombardi
Rojas-Lombardi at The Ballroom

Felipe Rojas-Lombardi's well-bred exterior might mislead you. You might not suspect that this is a man of strong, sure passions and a sense of adventure that constantly propels him to explore something new and to share it with others.

A native of Lima, Peru, who came to New York when he was eighteen, Rojas-Lombardi, now in his late thirties, spent several years working with James Beard, developing recipes for cookbooks, teaching cooking classes, and traveling. He then developed the food for Dean and DeLuca, the high-tech SoHo emporium that changed forever the way fine food is merchandised.

New Yorkers were in for another big change when Rojas-Lombardi took over at The Ballroom, a Chelsea cabaret-restaurant. His inspired idea was to open a *tapas* (appetizers) bar. In Spain, tapas bars are a way of life, convivial spots where people gather at the end of the day (and often at lunchtime) to enjoy a glass of Sherry, share local gossip, and nibble at a marvelous array of appetizers.

Rojas-Lombardi's version is a food lover's dream come true. Beneath a long rack hung with dried sausages, pheasant in plumage, and other seasonal delicacies, some two dozen dishes await: chicken *en escabèche*, served cold dressed with vinegar and tiny whole onions; a chunky vegetable caponata, a whole *jamón serrano*, the cured ham that is, according to the chef, "far superior to prosciutto—moister and less salty." There are plump snails in red beans, squid, and tender octopus in a sauce pungent with paprika. In all, there are more than two hundred tapas; guests choose a little of this, a little of that. Hot items include crisp roast suckling pig, grilled sausages and shrimp or wild mushrooms *al ajillo* or *a la plancha*.

Rojas-Lombardi has also devised a layered pie of fish and Swiss chard dramatically wrapped in pastry, and a moist 4-inch-high *tortilla española*, the potato omelet that might be considered a Spanish national dish. "No matter what else people order, they always have a little wedge of the tortilla," he says. "It's like bread—or if you stop to think about it, the fried egg and potato mixture is really just another version of the knish!"

The chef claims to be unable to discuss his cooking, then disproves his claim eloquently: "For me, food should look good, but with a minimum of garnish. A chicken should look like a chicken; a leek should look like a leek. You're enhancing the ingredients, not creating them. I try to figure out what is the minimum I can do to something to make it taste good—because the simpler you leave it, the fresher it will taste."

Chef Felipe Rojas-Lombardi

Menu

Pastel de Pescado
Savory pie of fish and Swiss chard

Cazuela de Chorizo
Spanish sausage stew with paprika and tomato sauce

Caracoles con Frijoles Colorados
Snails with red beans

Papas a la Arequipeña
Potato balls with roasted chilies, walnuts and cheese

Crema de Laurel
Caramel custard flavored with bay leaf

Pastel de Pescado

8 servings

Pastry
- *3 cups all purpose flour*
- *2 teaspoons salt*
- *Pinch of sugar*
- *1/2 cup (1 stick) unsalted butter, chilled and cut into small pieces*
- *1/4 cup (about) cold water*

Filling
- *2 large bunches Swiss chard (3 to 4 pounds total), coarsely chopped (about 6 quarts)*
- *2 tablespoons (1/4 stick) unsalted butter*
- *2 tablespoons olive oil*
- *2 small chilies, split lengthwise, trimmed, seeded and finely chopped*
- *3 garlic cloves, finely chopped*
- *1 teaspoon finely chopped fresh ginger*
- *1 medium onion, chopped*
- *Pinch each of freshly grated nutmeg, ground cumin, and dried thyme*
- *Juice of 1/2 lemon, or to taste*
- *Salt*

1 egg yolk mixed with 1
  teaspoon cold water
2 pounds fresh cod or other

firm white fish fillets
Pinch of black mustard
  seeds (optional)

1 *For pastry*: In mixing bowl or processor, combine flour, salt and sugar. Cut in ½ cup butter until crumbly. Add just enough cold water so that dough holds together in ball. Seal in plastic wrap and refrigerate at least 1 hour.

2 *For filling*: Working in batches, blanch Swiss chard in boiling salted water. Drain; rinse under cold water, and thoroughly squeeze dry. Chop finely and set aside.

3 Heat 2 tablespoons butter and oil in a large skillet. Add chilies, garlic and ginger and sauté over medium heat 1 minute without browning. Add onion and cook, stirring, until translucent. Add nutmeg, cumin and thyme and cook 1 minute longer. Add Swiss chard and stir until completely dry. Remove from heat, season to taste with lemon juice and salt, and set aside.

Counterclockwise from top: Papas a la Arequipeña, Pastel de Pescado, Cazuela de Chorizo, Caracoles con Frijoles Colorados and Crema de Laurel; in the center, a decorative arrangement of Papas a la Arequipeña.

4 To assemble, roll out dough on lightly floured work surface to very large circle ¼ inch thick. Fold into quarters and carefully transfer to buttered 9-inch springform pan. Unfold dough and gently fit it into bottom and sides of pan, leaving a generous overhang. Brush bottom and sides with some of egg yolk mixture; set aside to dry for about 10 minutes.

5 Preheat oven to 375°F. Spread half of Swiss chard filling over dough and arrange fish fillets on top. Cover evenly with remaining Swiss chard. Gently gather up edges of dough in center, and twist into a topknot, pinching knot with thumb and forefinger. Leaving a knot 2 to 3 inches high, cut off excess dough. Brush with remaining egg yolk mixture, sprinkle with mustard seeds, and cut several slashes around top.

6 Place on baking sheet and bake until golden, 1 to 1¼ hours. Cool completely on rack before removing sides of pan. Cut into wedges and serve at room temperature.

Cazuela de Chorizo

6 to 8 servings

Felipe Rojas-Lombardi prepares his Cazuela de Chorizo

3 tablespoons olive oil
1 medium onion, finely chopped
2 garlic cloves, finely chopped
½ teaspoon chopped fresh thyme or pinch of dried
½ bay leaf
7 links chorizo or other spicy sausage, thinly sliced
1 teaspoon paprika
1 teaspoon all purpose flour
¼ cup dry white wine
⅓ cup good-quality tomato sauce
⅓ cup water
8 small boiling potatoes, boiled and peeled
¼ cup chopped parsley

1 Heat oil in large skillet over medium heat. Add onion, garlic, thyme and bay leaf and cook, stirring, just until onion is translucent, about 5 minutes.

2 Add chorizo and sauté until golden brown, about 4 minutes. Add paprika and flour and stir to coat chorizo. Cook 2 to 3 minutes, pour in wine and cook briefly until it evaporates.

3 Stir in tomato sauce and water. Lower heat and simmer gently, uncovered, until sauce just coats chorizo, about 5 minutes. Serve hot over boiled potatoes. Sprinkle with parsley.

Caracoles con Frijoles Colorados

6 to 8 servings

4 tablespoons olive oil
2 tablespoons (¼ stick) unsalted butter
⅓ cup finely chopped shallot
2 garlic cloves, finely chopped
2 small fresh chilies, split lengthwise, seeded and finely chopped
Pinch of freshly grated nutmeg
Pinch of ground cloves
Pinch of ground cumin
1 can snails (6 or 7½ ounces), drained, rinsed and patted dry

2 tablespoons Pernod
1 cup beef stock (see recipe for Veal Stock, page 118) or water
4 cups cooked red kidney beans,* or 2 cans (about 1 pound each), drained and rinsed
½ cup chopped parsley
Salt and freshly ground pepper

1   Heat 2 tablespoons each of oil and butter in a large skillet over medium-high heat. Add shallot and garlic and sauté, stirring constantly, until lightly golden, about 3 minutes. Add chilies, nutmeg, cloves and cumin and stir 2 minutes.

2   Add snails and cook, stirring occasionally, 5 minutes. Add Pernod and cook until it evaporates.

3   Add beef stock, bring to boil and cook, stirring, 2 to 3 minutes. Add beans and ¼ cup parsley, stirring briefly just until beans are heated through. Remove from heat and stir in remaining 2 tablespoons olive oil and salt and pepper to taste. Sprinkle with remaining ¼ cup parsley and serve warm.

*To cook kidney beans, soak 1½ cups dried beans overnight in 4 cups of water. Drain, place in a pot with water to cover by 2 inches, and bring to a boil. Simmer, covered, over medium heat until tender.

Papas a la Arequipeña

6 to 8 servings

3 dried ancho chilies,* split lengthwise and seeded
⅓ cup annato seed*
1 cup vegetable oil

Potato Mixture
3 pounds potatoes (about 8 medium), peeled, cooked and mashed
Juice of 1 lime or lemon

*Available in Latin American markets.

Sauce

Coarse salt
1 cup olive oil
2 small fresh chilies, split lengthwise, seeded and coarsely chopped
1 garlic clove, peeled
1¼ cups walnuts (5 ounces)
2 teaspoons salt
½ pound Rumanian or Greek feta cheese, crumbled

Freshly ground pepper

Lettuce leaves
2 hard-cooked eggs, peeled and sliced
1 ear of corn, shucked, boiled until tender and thinly sliced through cob
¼ cup cilantro (coriander) leaves, chopped
Calamata olives (garnish)

1 Hold each chili with fork over gas flame, turning until lightly roasted on all sides. Place in bowl with 2 cups warm water; soak 20 minutes.

2 Prepare achiote oil by stirring together annato seeds and vegetable oil in saucepan over medium heat 2 minutes; remove from heat and cool. Oil will keep indefinitely, tightly covered, in a cool place.

Crema de Laurel

3   *For potato mixture*: Stir ¼ cup achiote oil into mashed potatoes (reserve remainder for another use). Add lime or lemon juice and salt to taste. Set aside.

4   *For sauce*: Drain ancho chilies, reserving soaking liquid, and place in processor with olive oil, fresh chilies and garlic. Process until smooth. With machine running, add ½ cup walnuts, ½ cup reserved pepper soaking liquid and 2 teaspoons salt; process until smooth. Add half of crumbled cheese and process until smooth. Transfer to small bowl. Coarsely chop remaining walnuts; add to mixture with remaining cheese, salt and pepper to taste.

5   Shape potato mixture into about 2 dozen 1½-inch balls. Arrange on lettuce leaves, spooning a little sauce on top. Garnish with eggs, corn, coriander and olives. Serve at room temperature.

Crema de Laurel

8 servings

Caramel
  1 cup sugar
  ¼ cup water
  1 bay leaf
  3 whole cloves

Custard
  8 egg yolks
  2 eggs

  1 cup sugar
  1 tablespoon amaretto or
    sweet Sherry
  4 cups milk
  1 cup whipping cream
  1 bay leaf

A caramelized bay leaf is placed on top of the baked Crema de Laurel

1   *For caramel*: Combine ingredients in small, heavy saucepan. Bring to boil over medium heat, stirring occasionally and brushing down any sugar crystals from side of pan with brush dipped in cold water. Continue to cook, without stirring, until syrup turns a medium amber color.

2   Immediately strain caramel (reserving bay leaf) into 12 x 4½ x 4-inch terrine or 9 x 5 x 3-inch loaf pan. Swirl rapidly to coat bottom and sides. Invert mold over parchment or waxed paper. Cool.

3   *For custard*: Preheat oven to 375°F. In large mixing bowl, whisk together egg yolks, eggs, sugar and amaretto until pale and light, about 3 minutes. Gently whisk in milk and cream. Strain into mold and place mold in roasting pan. Put pan on center rack of oven and place a bay leaf in center of custard. Add enough hot water to the roasting pan to come ⅓ of the way up the outside of the mold. Bake until just set, about 1 ½ hours (the 9 x 5 x 3-inch loaf pan may take slightly longer). Remove from water bath and cool to room temperature on rack. Refrigerate if desired. Place reserved caramelized bay leaf on top, slightly overlapping baked leaf. Serve cold or at room temperature.

André Soltner
Lutèce

Dining at Lutèce for the first time, many customers are taken aback to discover that the man who is generally considered to be the finest chef working in America today is not the august French character they would expect. Instead, they meet a shy, gentle man with a lilting Alsatian accent, whose boyish grin lights up his face as he realizes that his efforts have brought you real pleasure.

André Soltner's cooking might be likened to Mozart's music. Thoroughly grounded in classic tradition, he makes the classic new. He has a sure hand with meats, fish, pastry and sauces, and, like masters in all fields, knows well when not to do too much. In his veal en croûte in this menu, for example, Soltner lets the essential flavors speak for themselves: pale, tender veal medaillons creamy mushroom stuffing, crisp, buttery puff pastry, all moistened with a light *jus*.

In Soltner's hearty fish stews and superb dessert feuilletés of raspberries or oranges with caramel, he has the uncanny knack of balancing his flavorings just on the edge of excess, without ever going over. When he is at his best, Soltner's dishes are perfectly composed creations—his signature frozen raspberry soufflé in this menu is a masterful play of airy mousse, crunchy nut meringues, and intense raspberry sauce. And even when he works in a grand style—foie gras en brioche or the veal in this menu—his plates look spare and clean.

Born in the small Alsatian town of Thann, Soltner is the son of a cabinetmaker. He was brought to New York in 1961, at the age of twenty-eight, by André Surmain to open Lutèce. "I thought I'd come here, learn English, see what's what for a while, and then go back and open a business in France. Well, things don't work out the way we think." Named "*Meilleur Ouvrier de France*" as France's finest chef in 1968 (by which time he had become part-owner of Lutèce), Soltner bought out his partner in 1972, becoming *chef-propriétaire*. Though it is the tradition in most of the three-star restaurants in France, Soltner was one of the few chefs in America at that time to own and control his own restaurant.

Soltner is constantly evolving and experimenting with new dishes. "I just brought back some small pears from the country," he beams, referring to his home in the Catskills, where he skis on winter Sundays and plays tennis in summer. "I stuff them with praline and bake them in a soufflé. And I bring tomatoes and use them to make a *coulis* (thick puree), which I combine with a *beurre blanc* and serve with some excellent turbot. But you have to have real tomatoes, the kind that smell good."

Nothing pleases Soltner more than when customers trust him enough to leave the menu to him; granted this freedom, he

Chef André Soltner

orchestrates *dégustation* (tasting) menus of several courses served in small portions. "You see," he smiles, "between the guy in the kitchen and the guy in the dining room, there is an invisible string. You have to love him, you have to want to please him. I go around, and I see on people's faces that they're enjoying my food. Somebody asks, 'What's your secret?' There is no secret. People think we perform miracles. We don't—all we can do is cook with pride, and cook with love. And if I cook well, and the customer enjoys it and comes here and has a nice evening—*that's* a miracle!"

Menu

Potage au Potiron
Pumpkin soup served in a pumpkin shell

Sole à la Catalane
Paupiette of sole in a baked tomato, served with an herbed butter sauce

Médaillons de Veau en Croûte
Boneless loin of veal with a duxelles stuffing, wrapped in puff pastry and served with a light veal *jus*

Soufflé Glacé aux Framboises
Frozen raspberry mousse layered with crisp almond meringue, served with a fresh raspberry sauce

Potage au Potiron

6 servings

*1 ripe pumpkin, 8 to 10
inches in diameter*
*8 tablespoons (1 stick)
unsalted butter*
1 medium onion, chopped
⅔ cup dry white wine
*2 small white turnips, peeled
and sliced*
1 carrot, peeled and sliced

*6 cups Chicken Stock (about)
(see recipe, page 118)*
*Salt and freshly ground
white pepper*
*1 10-inch length of a narrow
baguette (French bread) or 2
small rolls, with crust,
thinly sliced*
½ cup whipping cream

1   Cut off and reserve top of pumpkin; use large spoon or melon baller to scoop out and discard all seeds and strings. Scrape out pumpkin flesh without breaking through shell. You should have about 6 cups of pumpkin pieces. Set aside hollow pumpkin and lid.

2   In large casserole, heat 2 tablespoons butter over medium heat. Add onion and sauté, stirring often, until softened and very lightly

Potage au Potiron

golden, about 6 minutes. Add wine and simmer 1 minute. Add turnips, carrot, reserved pumpkin flesh, and enough Chicken Stock to cover solids. Season lightly with salt and pepper. Cover and bring to boil.

3   Meanwhile, cut bread slices into thin wedges about ¹/₂ inch long. In large skillet, heat 3 tablespoons butter over medium heat. Add half of bread pieces and toss constantly in butter until lightly golden, about 5 minutes. Add these croutons to soup. Sauté remaining croutons in remaining butter; set aside for garnish.

4   Boil soup gently, covered, for 1 hour. Puree mixture in processor or blender until smooth. Return to clean saucepan, stir in cream, and bring to simmer. Thin, if necessary, with additional stock. Adjust seasoning with salt and pepper. Serve soup in pumpkin, passing remaining croutons separately.

Sole à la Catalane

This is one of the dishes that earned André Soltner the distinction "Meilleur Ouvrier de France" in 1968.

4 servings

4 medium-size ripe tomatoes
   Salt and freshly ground
   pepper
14 tablespoons (1³/₄ sticks)
   unsalted butter, cut into
   pieces, plus more as needed
4 small white onions, thinly
   sliced
2 fillets of sole, (about 6
   ounces each), split
   lengthwise

2 tablespoons finely chopped
   shallot
¹/₂ cup dry white wine
1 tablespoon chopped parsley
1 tablespoon chopped fresh
   chives

1   Preheat oven to 300°F. Carefully cut out core of each tomato, removing a small, narrow plug and leaving tomato intact. Blanch tomatoes in boiling water for a few seconds, drain under cold water and slip off skins. Cut a lid from smooth bottom of each tomato (opposite the core) and set aside. With melon scoop or spoon, carefully hollow out pulp and seeds from tomatoes, leaving neat shell. Place tomatoes and their lids in small buttered baking dish, sprinkle with salt and pepper, and set aside.

2   In small skillet, heat 2 tablespoons butter; sauté sliced onions over medium heat until softened but not browned, 5 to 7 minutes. Spoon onions into tomatoes, dividing evenly.

3   On a work surface, gently flatten sole fillets, tapping them with side of a wide knife blade. Carefully roll up each fillet, beginning with small (tail) end and with smooth, shiny skinned surface inside. Lightly butter heatproof shallow baking dish in which fillets will fit compactly. Scatter shallot into dish, then arrange rolled fish fillets over shallot. Salt and pepper fish lightly and pour wine over. Cover with buttered parchment or waxed paper, buttered side down. Place pan over medium heat and bring almost to boil. Place pan of fish and pan of tomatoes in oven. Bake until fillets are just cooked through, 6 to 8 minutes; *do not overcook.*

4 Remove pans from oven. With slotted spatula, lift each fillet, draining all liquid back into pan, and place each fillet upright in a tomato. Place pan of fish-cooking liquid over high heat and boil until reduced to few tablespoons of syrupy liquid. Reduce heat to very low. Whisk in remaining 12 tablespoons butter, 1 or 2 pieces at a time, adding more only when previous addition has become creamy and smooth. Strain this sauce into small bowl; stir in parsley and chives and season to taste with salt and pepper.

5 Place each stuffed tomato on warm serving plate. Spoon some sauce over each fillet and around each tomato. Gently replace lids and serve immediately.

Médaillons de Veau en Croûte

For this recipe, you may use either classic Puff Pastry (see recipe, page 119) or the quick puff pastry below. Chilling the veal and the stuffing thoroughly prevents them from overcooking and keeps the pastry crisp.

6 servings

Quick Puff Pastry

1 pound (4 cups) instant flour, plus more as needed
1 1/2 teaspoons salt
1 pound unsalted butter (4 sticks), cut into large chunks
3/4 cup cold water, (about)

Veal and Sauce

1 1/2 pounds boneless veal loin, well trimmed
Salt and freshly ground white pepper
All purpose flour
2 tablespoons (1/4 stick) unsalted butter
3 tablespoons chopped shallot
1/2 cup dry white wine
2 cups Veal Stock (see recipe, page 118)

Duxelles Stuffing

1 small pair calf's brains (10 to 12 ounces) (optional)
1/4 cup white wine vinegar (optional)
1 bay leaf (optional)
2 tablespoons (1/4 stick) unsalted butter
2 1/2 cups thinly sliced mushrooms (about 10 ounces)
Freshly ground black pepper
2 tablespoons chopped shallot
2 tablespoons chopped parsley

1 egg yolk beaten with 1 teaspoon cold water
Watercress sprigs (garnish)

1 *For quick puff pastry*: In mixing bowl or mixer, roughly combine flour, salt and butter, breaking up butter slightly (there should be visible chunks). Gradually add just enough cold water to hold the dough together; *do not overwork.*

2 Transfer dough to lightly floured work surface and roll it to rectangle about 9 × 12 inches. Dust board, dough, and rolling pin with flour as necessary to prevent sticking. Starting with closest short end, fold the dough into thirds as you would a letter. Rotate dough so open side is at your right. Repeat, rolling dough into rectangle, folding it into thirds and rotating it as before. Wrap the dough in plastic wrap and chill at least 1 hour.

3 Place dough on lightly floured work surface with open side at your right. Roll dough into rectangle as before. Now bring the two short ends together to meet in center of dough, then fold dough in half again toward you. Rotate ¼ turn, so open side is again at your right. Repeat, rolling dough into rectangle, folding in half, then in half again, and rotating ¼ turn. Wrap dough and chill again for at least 1 hour.

4 *For veal and sauce*: Cut loin of veal into 6 slices ½ to ¾ inches thick. Flatten slices slightly with cleaver or knife blade. Pat slices dry; sprinkle with salt and white pepper. Dredge slices in all purpose flour, shaking off excess to leave very light coating. In large skillet, heat 2 tablespoons butter over high heat. Add meat (work in batches if necessary) and sauté until golden, shaking pan occasionally and turning

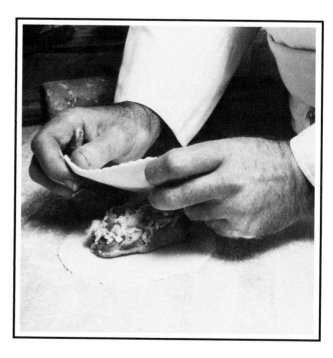

Duxelles-topped veal loin is wrapped in puff pastry for Médaillons de Veau en Croûte

Chef André Soltner and photographer Nancy McFarland

slices once, about 2 minutes. Lower heat to low, cover pan, and cook 2 minutes. Transfer meat to platter and pour off all but 1 tablespoon of butter from skillet. Add shallots, raise heat, and stir for 1 minute. Add wine, scraping up any browned bits in pan, and boil until reduced by half. Add Veal Stock and any juices from veal and boil until reduced by about ⅓. Strain sauce and set aside. Chill meat, covered.

5 For duxelles stuffing: If you are using calf's brains, soak brains in bowl of cold water with 2 tablespoons vinegar about 30 minutes. Drain; carefully remove as much membrane and veins as possible from brains. Set aside. In small saucepan, combine 3 cups cold water, remaining 2 tablespoons vinegar, a little salt and bay leaf. Bring to boil; simmer 10 minutes. Gently add brains and immediately remove pan from heat. Let brains sit in liquid, covered, 8 minutes; then transfer with slotted spatula to small bowl; set aside.

6 Heat 2 tablespoons butter in large skillet over medium-high heat. Add mushrooms, sprinkle with salt and black pepper, and stir until nearly dry, about 8 minutes. Add shallot and cook 2 minutes longer. Add cooked calf's brains and stir, breaking up brains, until mixture is almost pureed. Add ¼ cup of reserved Veal Stock mixture and simmer briefly until thick. Remove from heat; stir in parsley and adjust seasoning. Cool mixture completely; then chill, covered.

7 On lightly floured work surface, roll out about ⅓ of pastry into rectangular shape 1/16 inch thick. Cut 6 pastry ovals roughly the shape of veal medallions but somewhat larger, to leave a generous border. Roll out remaining pastry to large rectangle about ⅛ inch thick. Cut out 6 slightly larger pastry ovals, reserving trimmings for another use.

8 Place thinner set of pastry ovals on large ungreased baking sheet. Brush pastry lightly with egg yolk mixture, then place chilled veal medallion in center of each oval. Spread layer of cooled duxelles stuffing on each, mounding it slightly and dividing it evenly. Top each medallion with one of thicker pastry ovals, smoothing it gently without stretching. Press edges of pastry together firmly to seal. Brush pastry with egg wash. With large round cutter or knife, trim off edges of pastry, leaving ½-inch border. Use small knife to trace leaf pattern in top of each pastry; score a few lines along sides. Place baking sheet in refrigerator for 20 minutes or longer.

9 Preheat oven to 425°F. Bake veal en croûte on center rack of oven until golden brown, about 14 minutes. Meanwhile, reheat sauce, reducing it further if necessary until it coats a spoon lightly. Serve veal surrounded with some of sauce and garnished with watercress sprigs; serve remaining sauce separately.

Soufflé Glacé aux Framboises

8 Servings

Almond Meringue Layers
  2 egg whites
  ²/₃ cup ground blanched
    almonds
  ¹/₂ cup sugar

Mousse
  3 cups fresh raspberries or 3
    10-ounce packages frozen
    raspberries, thawed and
    drained (reserve liquid)

  ¹/₂ cup sugar
  3 tablespoons cold water
  1 tablespoon light corn syrup
  3 egg whites
    Juice of ¹/₂ lemon
  2 cups whipping cream

1 *For almond meringue layers*: Line baking sheet with parchment paper (or butter and flour it). Using pencil and 8-inch soufflé dish as guide, trace 2 circles exactly the diameter of dish onto parchment paper. Fold sheet of parchment or waxed paper in half lengthwise; lightly

Soufflé Glacé aux Framboises

oil one side of paper and wrap it around soufflé dish so it extends 3 inches above top of dish, taping it securely with masking tape.

2   Preheat oven to 200°F. Beat 2 egg whites until they form stiff peaks. Stir together ground almonds and sugar; gently fold into beaten egg whites. Transfer mixture to pastry bag fitted with round ½-inch tip. Starting in center and spiraling outward, form 2 8-inch circles ¼ inch thick. Bake until crisp, about 1½ hours. Cool on rack.

3   *For mousse*: Choose a few perfect raspberries for garnish and set aside. Puree remaining raspberries in processor or blender until very smooth. Transfer 2 tablespoons of puree, with seeds, to measuring cup. Strain remaining puree into mixing bowl, eliminating all seeds. Add enough strained puree to the 2 tablespoons to measure ½ cup. Set aside. Chill remaining strained puree, which will be used as sauce.

4   In small, heavy saucepan combine sugar, water and corn syrup. Bring slowly to boil over medium heat, stirring occasionally and brushing down any sugar crystals from sides of pan with brush dipped in cold water. Raise heat slightly and cook until temperature of syrup reaches 240°F (soft ball stage). While syrup is cooking, beat 3 egg whites in mixer until stiff. As soon as syrup reaches 240°F, lower mixer speed to slow and pour hot syrup onto beaten whites in very thin stream. When all of syrup has been incorporated, raise mixer speed and beat meringue until cool.

5   Stir together the ½ cup reserved raspberry puree and lemon juice; fold into meringue until nearly blended. Whip cream until stiff; fold into meringue until blended; *do not overmix*.

6   To assemble, spread ¾-inch layer of mousse in prepared soufflé dish. Carefully peel off paper from a meringue layer and place layer on top. Repeat, adding ¾-inch layer of mousse, then remaining meringue layer. Top with remaining mousse, smoothing it gently with spatula. Freeze at least 3 hours.

7   To serve, carefully remove paper collar. Smooth exposed edge of soufflé, if necessary, with metal spatula. Use knife blade or long metal spatula to score shallow crisscross pattern in top of soufflé. Garnish with reserved raspberries. Serve in wedges, spooning a little of chilled raspberry puree around each portion and serving remainder separately.

Simon Teng
Auntie Yuan

At Auntie Yuan, traditional Chinese delicacies are reinterpreted in a sleek setting that highlights the clean, light flavors, crisp textures and artful simplicity of the cuisine. As devised by co-owner Ed Schonfeld and interpreted by Chinese master chef Simon Teng, the food is a revelation: presented in high style but rich with the essential flavors of Chinese home cooking.

David Keh, the elder statesman of Chinese restaurateurs in New York, co-owns the restaurant with Ed Schonfeld, a Jew from Brooklyn who speaks "fluent restaurant Chinese" and understands Chinese regional cuisines better than some Chinese.

The concept for Auntie Yuan was to personalize Chinese cooking by presenting a Chinese grandma's cooking in a restaurant setting. Four women were brought from China (one of whom really was called Auntie Yuan). Schonfeld tasted his way through their repertoires, as well as that of Teng, choosing what he thought was exciting or special. The result was a synthesis of Chinese home cooking, restaurant cooking and food from the traditional Chinese banquet, where many courses are presented in sequence, in small portions for tasting.

A meal at Auntie Yuan begins with cold appetizers and an exciting array of hot ones, such as the pork-filled dumplings in spicy sesame sauce. Watching Teng roll out and fill the crescent-shaped pockets is exhilarating; he moves at lightning speed and smiles as visitors watch him shape the supple dough with only a miniature rolling pin and his deft fingers.

Next comes a cold salad of roast duck on a bed of crisp rice noodles. Teng seems to love showing how the noodles "explode" in hot oil in less than 10 seconds.

The steamed salmon that follows is an unorthodox adaptation. In the traditional Chinese kitchen, fish is steamed whole, with the shredded vegetables placed on top, not in small geometric portions, as here. ("There is also no salmon in China," Schonfeld confesses. "But there's no real sea bass either—and that's on every Chinese menu in New York. The point is to get something that's fresh and local and nice.")

We then move into the main course, an authentically home-style chicken. Teng flies between three deep woks, sizzling spinach in one, frying the chicken, then glazing it in a piquant, shiny sauce in seconds. The result is a masterpiece of bright colors: twice-fried chicken offset by a moist, tender bed of spinach, the tart sauce cutting through the oil-crisped coating.

Wine by the glass and other untraditional aspects of dining at Auntie Yuan, such as the elegance of Wedgwood and cloisonné service plates, sometimes surprise guests, who find to their pleasure that under Schonfeld and Teng's care, they are in for a feast that is true to the Chinese adage: "To eat well requires an adventurous spirit."

Chef Simon Teng (right) with Ed Schonfeld and maitre d' Craig Chow

Menu

Spicy Dumplings with Sesame Sauce and Hot Oil

Boiled pork-filled dumplings served with a spicy sesame sauce and drizzled with hot chili oil

Auntie Yuan Duck Salad

Cold shredded roast duck on a bed of lettuce and crisp-fried rice noodles, with a spicy mustard dressing

Steamed Salmon with Black Bean Sauce

Fillet of salmon topped with a julienne of red and green peppers, ginger and black beans, steamed in soy sauce and sesame oil

Home-style Chicken

Crisp stir-fried chicken in a pungent soy-vinegar sauce, served on a bed of spinach

Spicy Dumplings with Sesame Sauce and Hot Oil

4 servings
(24 to 30 dumplings)

Dough
  2 cups all purpose flour
    Pinch of salt
  $^1/_2$ to $^3/_4$ cup cold water (about)

Filling
  2 tablespoons cold water
  1 tablespoon finely chopped
    fresh ginger

1 tablespoon finely chopped
  scallion
$^1/_2$ pound ground pork butt
$^1/_4$ teaspoon salt
  Pinch of freshly ground
  white pepper

Spicy Sesame Sauce
  1/3 cup plus 1 tablespoon tahini
    (sesame seed paste)
  1/3 cup Chinese rice vinegar
  1/3 cup good-quality soy sauce
  1/4 cup sugar
  1 1/2 tablespoons Oriental sesame
    oil

  1 tablespoon finely chopped
    garlic
  1 tablespoon hot chili oil
  1/2 teaspoon freshly ground
    Szechwan peppercorns

  Hot chili oil
  Sliced scallions

1 For dough: In a mixer or processor, combine flour and salt. Gradually add water and knead to form a firm but moist dough. Wrap and refrigerate 2 hours or more.

2 For filling: Combine water with ginger and scallion. Let stand, covered, 2 hours or longer. Strain, reserving liquid. Stir liquid into ground pork with salt and pepper. Cover and refrigerate until needed.

3 For spicy sesame sauce: Use a processor or blender to combine sauce ingredients. Set aside.

4 To assemble, divide dough into 4 pieces. Roll each piece into cylinder about 1 inch in diameter. Pinch or cut 6 or 7 walnut-size pieces from each cylinder. Dust pieces with flour and stand each on a cut side. Use rolling pin to flatten into 2 1/2 to 3-inch circles, turning them with your fingers as you roll and making them slightly thicker in center than at edges.

5 Place rounded teaspoon of meat filling in center of each circle. Fold edges up over filling, pressing dough together in center, then on two sides. Pinch firmly. Place on floured sheet of waxed paper.

6 Cook in large pot of boiling water until meat is firm, 4 to 5 minutes. Drain and transfer to serving bowls. Drizzle with spicy sesame sauce and a few drops of chili oil. Sprinkle with scallions and serve.

Auntie Yuan Duck Salad

4 servings

Roast Duck
  1 4 1/2- to 5-pound duckling,
    excess fat removed
  1 tablespoon soy sauce
  1/2 teaspoon salt
  1/2 teaspoon coarsely ground
    Szechwan peppercorns
  2 tablespoons honey
  2 tablespoons Chinese rice
    vinegar

Dressing
  1 teaspoon dry mustard
    Salt and freshly ground
    white pepper
  2 teaspoons sugar
  1/2 teaspoon finely chopped
    garlic
  1 1/2 tablespoons soy sauce

Spicy Dumplings with Sesame Sauce and Hot Oil

¹/₃ cup Chicken Stock (see recipe, page 118)
¹/₃ cup Chinese rice vinegar
¹/₃ cup vegetable oil

Vegetable oil (for deep frying)
3¹/₂ ounces mai fun (rice sticks)

2 cups shredded iceberg lettuce
6 tablespoons slivered scallions (garnish)
Cilantro (coriander) (garnish)
1 teaspoon sesame seed, lightly toasted

1   *For roast duck*: Preheat oven to 400°F. Rub soy sauce, salt and pepper into cavity of duck; place duck on rack in roasting pan. Stir together honey and vinegar and brush some over duck. Roast until crisp and golden, about 1 hour, occasionally brushing with honey-vinegar mixture. Cool.

2   With sharp knife, remove skin from each side of breast and cut into thin slivers. Remove meat from each side of breast and cut into thin slivers. Combine skin and slivered duck; reserve 1 cup; save remainder for another use.

3   *For dressing*: In small bowl, blend together dressing ingredients and set aside.

4   In wok or wide casserole, heat 2 inches vegetable oil over high heat to 450°F. Carefully add mai fun noodles; in a few seconds they will puff. Turn carefully with a skimmer and cook other side. Remove and drain on paper towels.

5   Break up noodles and arrange on 4 chilled serving plates. Scatter shredded lettuce over and top with reserved duck. Garnish with scallions and cilantro. Stir dressing and drizzle small amount over each salad. Sprinkle with sesame seeds and serve, passing remaining dressing separately.

Steamed Salmon with Black Bean Sauce

2 servings

2 salmon fillets, skin removed
   (*about 4 ounces each*)
1 red bell pepper
1 green bell pepper
2 tablespoons shredded
   bamboo shoots
2 teaspoons fermented black
   beans
12 matchstick-thin slivers fresh
   ginger

4 teaspoons shredded scallion
   (*white portion only*)
2 tablespoons soy sauce
1 tablespoon Chicken Stock
   (*see recipe, page 118*)
   Pinch of freshly ground
   white pepper
   Dash of vegetable oil
   Dash of Oriental sesame oil

1   If fillets are thicker than $1/2$ to $5/8$ inch, carefully cut in half horizontally (as you would an English muffin). Trim each into a neat 4-inch square.

2   Cut off tops and bottoms of peppers to leave a band about 2 inches wide; remove seeds and ribs. Cut two 4-inch-long rectangular pieces from each. Cut into $1/8$-inch julienne, leaving pieces grouped in a neat rectangle. Place salmon on an oiled steamer tray or plate. Use cleaver or knife blade to transfer pepper rectangles to fish, completely covering each fillet.

3   Scatter bamboo shoots over fish, then sprinkle with black beans, ginger and scallions. In small bowl, stir together soy sauce, chicken stock, white pepper, vegetable oil and sesame oil. Pour mixture over.

4   Steam in covered steamer (making sure that water boils steadily but does not boil away) until just cooked through and opaque, 5 to 8 minutes (timing varies according to thickness of fish). Carefully transfer to serving plate, spoon sauce around and serve immediately.

Home-style Chicken

2 servings

Chicken

- 2 chicken legs with thigh attached (1 to 1¼ pounds total)
- ¼ teaspoon salt
- ¼ teaspoon freshly ground white pepper
- 1 tablespoon Chinese rice wine or *dry Sherry*
- 1 tablespoon plus 1 teaspoon beaten egg
- 1 tablespoon cornstarch
- 1 tablespoon peanut or vegetable oil

Sauce

- ⅓ cup Chicken Stock (see recipe, page 118)
- 1 teaspoon cornstarch
- 1 teaspoon Chinese rice wine or *dry Sherry*
- 1 teaspoon soy sauce
- ½ teaspoon Chinese rice vinegar
- ½ teaspoon sugar

Finishing Mixture

- 4 teaspoons Chinese rice vinegar
- 1 tablespoon Chinese rice wine or *dry Sherry*
- 2 teaspoons Oriental sesame oil

Spinach

- 2 tablespoons peanut or vegetable oil
- 3 cups whole spinach leaves, large stems removed
- ¼ cup Chicken Stock
- ¼ teaspoon finely chopped garlic
- ¼ teaspoon salt

- 2½ cups (about) peanut or vegetable oil
- 2 garlic cloves, thinly sliced
- 2 tablespoons sliced scallion
- ½ teaspoon finely chopped fresh ginger

Boned chicken pieces are twice-fried for Home-style Chicken

1 *For chicken*: Hold each chicken portion by end of leg and use kitchen towel to grab skin at thigh end. Pull off skin and discard. With sharp boning or paring knife, slit leg and thigh meat, cutting parallel to bones. Scrape thigh meat away from bone. Cut through joint between leg and thigh. Scrape away all remaining thigh meat and cut or pull out bone. Use cleaver to cut off knob end of leg. Scrape meat from leg bone and pull out bone. Place each boned piece of chicken, skinned side down, on work surface and break up tendons by scoring meat with cleaver. Cut into 1½-inch pieces and transfer to small bowl.

2 Sprinkle chicken with salt, pepper and rice wine. Stir in beaten egg, sprinkle with cornstarch and toss to combine. Drizzle with oil, toss, cover and refrigerate at least 1 hour.

3 *For sauce*: In small bowl stir together a little of stock and the cornstarch. Add remaining sauce ingredients and set aside.

4 *For finishing mixture*: Blend together ingredients in small bowl and set aside.

Home-style Chicken

5 *For spinach*: In wok or large skillet, heat oil until nearly smoking. Add spinach, stock, garlic and salt and stir-fry until just wilted, 1 to 1½ minutes. Arrange in large ring on warm serving plates.

6 To assemble, in second wok or skillet, heat oil to 360°F (a piece of garlic will sizzle steadily when placed in oil). Add chicken pieces, separating them with skimmer, and fry, turning once or twice, until lightly golden, 2 to 3 minutes. Remove and drain on paper towels. Raise heat of oil to 400°F and return chicken to wok. Fry until golden brown, about 1 minute; remove and drain. Pour off all but 1 tablespoon oil. Add garlic, scallions and ginger and cook about 30 seconds. Add sauce, then chicken and toss to coat. Add finishing mixture, tossing to combine. Arrange chicken on spinach and serve immediately.

Alfredo Viazzi
Café Domel

New York can boast of more fine Italian restaurants than anywhere except Italy, from high-toned East Side spots, where a waiter in black tie tosses your linguine tableside, to Little Italy havens of *cucina casalinga* ("housewife-style cooking"), with plenty of red sauce and garlic.

But for several years now, those who are in the know have beaten a path to the door of the Trattoria da Alfredo, a tiny, no-frills spot on the western fringes of Greenwich Village.

Here, everyone from Mayor Ed Koch to James Beard to neighbors from down the street can be found, boisterously enjoying such lusty dishes as tortellini della nonna with cream, prosciutto and peas, soothing pasta with tomatoes and ricotta cheese, cotechino sausage and vegetables with a lively green herb sauce, and Gino Cofacci's mocha Dacquoise.

Alfredo Viazzi, for whom the place was named, might be said to have introduced this city to the entire concept of dining in a trattoria, the kind of small place found in every town in Italy, where locals know that the food is plentiful and freshly prepared, the wines robust and easy to get down, and the welcome friendly. In a city where atmosphere can make or break a restaurant, Viazzi chose to keep his comfortable room simple and let his cooking speak for itself.

It worked. Viazzi now oversees several neighborhood restaurants, including his latest, Café Domel. He sees the cafe in the tradition of the European coffeehouse; guests can order anything from "a little something"—appetizers, pasta, coffee and pastry—to a full meal. The food here is a creative hybrid of old Vienna and Morocco (where Viazzi lived for over a year), plus northern Italian pastas; upstairs, his wife, actress Jane White, has opened a boutique.

People come back to Viazzi's restaurants because of the spirit of the man himself: outspoken, theatrical, passionate. "Food," he explains in his recent cookbook memoir, *Cucina e Nostalgia* (Random House), "has played such an important role in my life that it became the protagonist and I the bit player. I come from a country [he was born in Savona, Italy] where food is the topic of all conversation; while seated at lunch we seriously discuss what we will eat at dinner that night. '*Una bella mangiata, il giornale, un espresso, sigarette, una discussione politica, una bella donna accanto* [A wonderful dinner, the newspaper, an espresso, cigarettes, a political discussion and the company of a beautiful woman].'"

Viazzi's cooking is simple and hearty. The veal roast in this menu, for example, could not be easier; it is essentially a pot roast. But the pancetta, garlic, almonds and dried porcini mushrooms transform it into something memorable. And the Tortel-

Chef Alfredo Viazzi

loni di Zucca, folded pasta pockets filled with a delicate and unusual mixture of mashed cooked squash studded with bits of escarole, ham and grated Parmesan cheese, is a recipe Viazzi learned from Chef Gino Ratti, "a first-class chef and despicable miser...who taught me all I know of the art of cooking, the quality of food and wines."

The Marsala-laced fritters that conclude this menu are "the kind of dessert that might be made at home," the chef explains. "Very few Italians bake their own desserts." These dishes, while simple, all have the flair that marks everything Viazzi does (he even wears an ascot while he cooks). And that flair is just what once prompted James Beard to dub this chef's cooking "Italian cooking—with an Alfredo Viazzi accent."

Menu

Minestra di Piselli Freschi e Carciofi
Fresh pea and artichoke soup

Tortelloni di Zucca
Squash-filled tortelloni with tomato-cream sauce

Vitello Contadina
Farmer-style veal, cooked in casserole with pancetta, porcini and almonds

Frittelle di Corleone
Corleone-style fritters with Marsala and raisins

Minestra di Piselli Freschi e Carciofi

Minestra di Piselli Freschi e Carciofi

6 servings

4 very small artichokes
  Juice of 1 lemon

6 cups Chicken Stock (see
  recipe, page 118)
6 tablespoons (³/₄ stick)
  unsalted butter
4 large garlic cloves, finely
  chopped

¹/₄ teaspoon salt
  Freshly ground pepper
1 tablespoon chopped parsley
¹/₂ cup fresh peas or frozen
  peas, thawed
  Freshly grated Parmesan or
  pecorino cheese

1 Trim off all tough outer leaves from artichokes. Cut off tops of artichokes; trim and peel bottoms, leaving a little of stem. Quarter artichokes. (If using larger artichokes, scrape away the fuzzy choke.) Toss with lemon juice.

2 Heat chicken stock to simmer in medium saucepan. Heat butter in skillet. Add artichokes, garlic, and salt and pepper. Sauté, tossing over medium-high heat 5 minutes. Using a slotted spoon, transfer artichokes and garlic to simmering stock. Add parsley and simmer, covered, 15 minutes. Uncover; add peas and simmer 5 minutes longer. Serve hot with grated Parmesan or pecorino cheese.

Tortelloni di Zucca

4 to 6 servings

Pasta
- *3 cups all purpose flour*
- *3 eggs, lightly beaten*
- *1¹/₂ teaspoons olive oil*
- *2 tablespoons water (about)*

Filling
- *1 acorn squash (about 1³/₄ pounds)*
- *1 cup escarole leaves*
- *1¹/₂ tablespoons butter*
- *¹/₃ cup freshly grated Parmesan cheese*
- *1 tablespoon chopped parsley*
- *¹/₄ cup chopped Black Forest or other ham*
- *¹/₄ cup ricotta cheese*

- *1 egg*
- *Freshly ground black pepper*
- *Generous pinch of freshly grated nutmeg*
- *Salt to taste*

Tomato-Cream Sauce
- *¹/₄ cup (¹/₂ stick) unsalted butter*
- *1 cup whipping cream*
- *Freshly ground white pepper*
- *¹/₃ cup grated pecorino cheese*
- *¹/₄ cup good-quality tomato sauce*
- *Freshly grated Parmesan cheese*

Alfredo Viazzi cuts up the acorn squash for his Tortelloni di Zucca

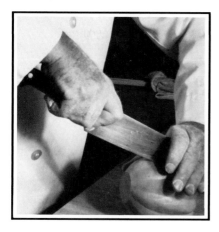

1 *For pasta:* In mixer with dough hook, or processor, combine flour, eggs and oil, adding water as needed to form a soft ball. Transfer to lightly floured work surface and knead about 5 minutes. Cover with cloth and set aside for 30 minutes.

2 *For filling:* Halve squash; remove all seeds and strings. Cut into large wedges and cook, covered, in boiling salted water until tender, about 12 minutes. Drain, cool briefly and scoop flesh from skin (you should have about 2 cups).

3 Place escarole in a saucepan with about 1 cup water; cover. Steam, tossing once or twice, just until wilted, 3 to 5 minutes. Drain in colander, rinse with cold water, squeeze dry and chop coarsely. Set aside.

4 Melt 1¹/₂ tablespoons butter in a large skillet over medium-high heat. Add squash and cook, stirring, until dry, about 5 minutes, breaking up the flesh coarsely as it cooks. Add Parmesan and parsley, lower heat to medium and stir 3 minutes. Transfer mixture to mixing bowl and stir in escarole, ham, ricotta and egg. Season with black pepper, nutmeg and a little salt, if desired. Set aside.

5 To assemble, cut dough in 3 pieces. Roll each piece with heavy rolling pin on lightly floured board (or use a pasta machine) until ¹/₈ inch thick (you should be able to see your fingers through the dough). Use a 4-inch cutter to cut out rounds of dough; place them on lightly floured baking sheet. Place about 1¹/₂ teaspoons squash filling on lower half of each round, leaving a border. Fold top half of each round over filling and press edges together to seal. Wrap edges of each half-circle around your index finger, bringing ends together to overlap by about ¹/₄ inch. Pinch edges to seal.

6 *For sauce*: Melt ¹/₄ cup butter in heavy saucepan. Add cream and a generous amount of white pepper, whisking over medium-high heat. Stir in pecorino and tomato sauce. Boil gently 3 to 4 minutes.

7 Meanwhile, cook tortelloni in large pot of boiling salted water until they float to surface, then boil 1 minute longer; drain. Place in heated serving bowls, nap with sauce and serve immediately, with additional Parmesan and white pepper.

Vitello Contadina

6 servings

3 to 3¹/₂ *pounds top round of
  veal in 1 piece, trimmed*
2 *small sprigs fresh rosemary
  or* ³/₄ *teaspoon dried*
8 *ounces sliced pancetta
  (Italian dry-cured unsmoked
  bacon) or bacon*
2 *tablespoons chopped parsley*
2 *bay leaves
  Freshly grated nutmeg
  Coarsely ground pepper*
1 *ounce dried porcini
  mushrooms, soaked in hot
  water to cover for 20 to 30
  minutes (reserve soaking
  liquid)*

6 *tablespoons (³/₄ stick)
  unsalted butter*
3 *garlic cloves, peeled
  Salt*
¹/₂ *cup dry white wine*
¹/₂ *cup dry vermouth*
¹/₃ *cup coarsely ground
  almonds*

1 Make deep incision down center of veal, being careful not to cut all the way through; gently open it out flat as you would a book. Trim off and reserve any irregular pieces of meat along edges, leaving a neat, compact shape.

2 Place rosemary along center of meat, then top with half of pancetta, overlapping slices. Sprinkle with parsley and top with remaining pancetta, bay leaves, nutmeg and pepper. Drain porcini, reserving and straining liquid. Rinse porcini, drain again, chop coarsely and place on top of meat. Top with any reserved meat trimmings. Close up meat compactly and tie with kitchen twine, going once around lengthwise and several times around crosswise. Pat dry.

3 Melt butter in deep casserole over medium heat. Add garlic and cook until golden, about 6 minutes; discard garlic. Add stuffed roast, season with salt, and cook until lightly golden on all sides, 15 to 20 minutes.

4 Add wine and vermouth, basting meat. Cover casserole, lower heat to medium low and cook, turning and basting occasionally, for 15 min-

Fritelle di Corleone

utes. Stir in almonds and ½ cup of reserved mushroom-soaking liquid. Cook, turning and basting occasionally, until tender, about 15 to 20 minutes longer.

5 Transfer meat to carving board and let stand 10 minutes or longer. Boil sauce until lightly reduced. Cut roast into ½-inch-thick slices; if necessary, reheat slices in casserole. Spoon sauce over and serve.

Frittelle di Corleone

6 servings

¼ cup golden raisins
½ cup Marsala or sweet Sherry

2 egg yolks
½ cup milk

1 cup all purpose flour
Pinch of salt

Vegetable oil (for frying)
Powdered sugar

1 Soak raisins in Marsala 30 minutes.

2 Drain raisins, reserving wine. Put flour and salt in mixing bowl. Stirring very gently with wooden spoon, gradually blend in wine until smooth. Stir in egg yolks and just enough milk to bring batter to consistency of thick cream sauce. Stir reserved raisins into batter.

3 In a large skillet, heat 1 inch of oil to 375°F. Using about 3 tablespoons for each fritter, spoon batter into oil; *do not crowd*. Fry until golden, turning once, 4 to 5 minutes. Drain on paper towels; repeat with remaining batter. Dust with powdered sugar and serve hot.

Basic Preparations

Chicken Stock

Makes 3 to 4 quarts

5 pounds chicken parts
(backs, necks, carcasses and
giblets [no livers])
Cold water
2 large onions, coarsely
chopped
2 carrots, peeled, trimmed and
coarsely chopped
2 celery stalks, with leaves,
trimmed and coarsely
chopped

2 garlic cloves, crushed
1 small bunch parsley stems
2 sprigs fresh thyme or large
pinch dried
1 bay leaf
1/2 teaspoon coarse salt
6 peppercorns

1   Wash chicken parts well and place in large stockpot; add cold water to cover by about 2 inches. Bring slowly to boil, skimming all froth from surface.

2   Lower heat and add all remaining ingredients except peppercorns. Simmer, uncovered, 3 hours; add water as needed just to cover ingredients; skim when necessary. Add peppercorns for last 15 minutes.

3   Strain into large bowl through colander lined with double layer of dampened cheesecloth. Gently press solids to extract all liquid; discard solids. Cool to room temperature and refrigerate. When chilled, lift off solidified fat and discard. Pour stock into containers for storage; label and date. Stock keeps 3 days in refrigerator, 6 months in freezer.

Veal Stock

For beef stock, follow same procedure, using all beef bones.

Makes about 2 quarts

2 tablespoons vegetable oil
6 pounds meaty veal bones
and knuckles or
combination of veal and
beef bones
2 medium onions, trimmed
and quartered (do not peel)

2 carrots, peeled, trimmed and
coarsely chopped
2 celery stalks, trimmed and
coarsely chopped
1 leek (white and green parts),
trimmed, halved lengthwise,
and coarsely chopped

4 garlic cloves (do not peel)
1 small bunch parsley stems

*2 cups water, plus more as
needed*
*2 ripe fresh or canned
tomatoes, cored and coarsely
chopped*

*3 branches fresh thyme or ¹/₂
teaspoon dried*
2 bay leaves
2 whole cloves
³/₄ teaspoon coarse salt
8 whole peppercorns

1 Preheat oven to 450°F. Put oil in roasting pan and heat briefly in oven. Add bones; toss to coat and roast 35 minutes. Add onions, carrots, celery, leek, garlic and parsley stems, tossing to coat with fat. Roast 30 minutes longer.

2 Remove pan from oven and transfer bones and vegetables to clean stockpot, draining off as much fat as possible. Place roasting pan over medium-high heat (use 2 burners if necessary), add 2 cups cold water and boil briefly, scraping up all browned bits. Transfer liquid to stockpot and add enough cold water to cover. Bring slowly to boil, skimming off all possible froth.

3 Lower heat and add tomatoes, thyme, bay leaves, cloves and salt. Simmer uncovered 6 to 8 hours, adding water as needed just to cover ingredients; skim when necessary. Add peppercorns for last 15 minutes.

4 Strain into a large bowl through colander lined with double layer of dampened cheesecloth. Gently press solids to extract all liquids; discard solids. Cool to room temperature and refrigerate. When chilled, lift off solidified fat and discard. Pour into containers for storage; label and date. Stock keeps 3 days in refrigerator, 6 months in freezer.

Puff Pastry

Makes about 2¹/₂ pounds

*1 pound all purpose flour
(3¹/₂ to 4 cups)*
1¹/₂ teaspoons salt
1 pound (4 sticks) unsalted

*butter, chilled and cut into
pieces*
1 cup cold water (about)

1 Set aside about ¹/₂ cup flour on work surface. Place remaining flour with salt in mixing bowl or mixer. Add ¹/₄ cup (¹/₂ stick) butter and cut mixture together until crumbly. Add just enough cold water so mixture can be gathered together in ball. Cut a cross in top of ball, place in covered bowl and chill about 30 minutes.

2   Place remaining butter on work surface with reserved flour; toss to coat. Use heel of hand to work flour into butter. Place butter-flour mixture on sheet of waxed paper, cover with second sheet and press mixture into flat square. Refrigerate just until butter-flour mixture is approximately same consistency as refrigerated dough.

3   Roll dough into a cloverleaf shape, with 4 "leaves" extending diagonally from center. Place butter-flour mixture in center; then fold each "leaf" over, forming a neat, square package with the leaves slightly overlapping.

4   Roll dough on lightly floured surface to large rectangle with short end toward you. Fold into thirds, as you would a letter. Rotate dough ¼ turn, so open side is at right (this is called a single turn). Repeat, rolling dough into large rectangle, folding into thirds and rotating ¼ turn. Wrap dough and chill 1 hour or longer.

5   Give dough 2 more sets of 2 single turns, always beginning and ending with open side at right. Refrigerate 1 hour or longer between each set of 2 turns. After final set of turns (6 single turns in all), wrap and refrigerate dough again for at least 1 hour.

Clarified Butter

Cut any amount of unsalted butter into pieces and melt slowly in saucepan. Skim off as much foam as possible from surface. Carefully pour off all clear golden liquid (this is the clarified butter), leaving all milky residue in bottom of pan (discard residue). Clarified butter keeps well, tightly sealed, in refrigerator or freezer. One-half pound butter (2 sticks) yields about ¾ cup clarified butter.